A DAM KIDS' MEMORIES OF THE AUSABLE RIVER

Growing up in the 1940s and 1950s

To Kathy
Donna Janice Emerick

Donna Janice Emerick
Copyright 2019

Dedicated To

Donald and Helen Weinberg, Mom and Dad; and
Robert L. Emerick, husband for 61 Years

Donald, Janice & Helen Weinberg

Robert Emerick & Janice Weinberg in front of Dam house at Loud Dam. Water was usually sixteen feet deep.

The AuSable River

THE RIVER

The river runs for miles
With a wandering life of its own.
It shows its awesome power
And always calls me home.

In my youth, it was my friend
When I was older, it spurred me on.
It gave me life before I knew it
And to it, again, I will roam.

My life has shown me many things
That have molded and shaped me in part
But the river has constantly stood by my side
And calls me to hear its heart.

By Susan M. Maturen, 2003
For Mother, who grew up on the AuSable River

TABLE OF CONTENTS

Dedication 2
The River 5
Prologue 8
Introduction 10
Chapter 1: Memories   12
Chapter 2: Flint and Family 28
Chapter 3: Company House 37
Chapter 4: Dams 44
Safety on the Dam 51
River Water and Dams 52
Roads 54
Chapter 5: On My Own 63
At First 68
Enter Suzie 70
Hair Perms 72
Chapter 6: Starting School 74
School Clothes 77
Chapter 7: WWII and Hard Times 79
Chapter 8: The Big Hill and Jesus 89
Chapter 9: The Woods 92
Eagles 103
Chapter 10: Making Do 104
Mom's Cakes 107
The Chocolate Escapade 108
Raising Chickens 109
Chapter 11: Riding the School Bus 115
Chapter 12: Snakes 121

Chapter 13: Friends and Fun Recess 128
Music-Piano-Band 129
Phone Calls and Female Trouble 132
Dad's Model-T 133
Sledding, Ice Skating 135
Swimming 137
Roller Skating 138
Horses 139
Radio/TV 142
Movies 144
Polio's Effects 145
Chapter 14: Fishing, Trapping, and Hunting 156
Partridge Hunting, Deer Hunting 162
Chapter 15: Summer Job 173
Distance, Driving, Cottage/Summer People 175
Canoe Races 178
High School and Teachers 179
Chapter 16: Bob 182
Chapter 17: Peggy the Dog 190
Going Away but Coming Back 191
Chapter 18: Endings 194
Epilogue 196
Afterward 198
Lumberman's Monument 200
Maps 202, 203
Acknowledgements and Thank You 204
Research 206

Prologue

The Mighty AuSable

Many things have changed over my lifetime like increased population and housing in the Oscoda area, new stores, cells phones and computers were invented. The AuSable River has changed too. Her banks have moved and shifted over time, her cabins have increased in size, been demolished or have been remodeled into full sized homes. Some of the same trees still line the ever-flowing River. Looking at her recently from River Road, I saw the same river as when I rode by in a school bus morning and night, kindergarten to twelfth grade, spring, fall, and winter.

The River would put on her winter coat from late fall until spring, keeping the same spirit of life living within her waters through the changing seasons. I always feel that spirit when I cross her bridges, from Grayling in the west to Oscoda in the east, and I feel it even more when my feet or hands are in her waters. I always have!

The AuSable River has run millions of gallons of water and generated millions of kilowatts of power through the dams. The River drains a large mass of land on each side of her banks. That drainage, from seeping springs to large creeks, flows into the main River. When it rains, the water flows faster than ever.

The AuSable can be moody. She can be gentle. She calms me, heals my body and soul, even as she continues to run, deep, wide, and sometimes furiously to Lake Huron. To me, she never seems to change. To me, she is the Mighty AuSable River.

INTRODUCTION

This book is about the life of a girl who grew up on the AuSable River in Michigan during the 1940's and 1950's. What I lived like in those two decades will never be the same again. My story involves company housing, hydro operations, dams, and my daily life growing up on the AuSable River. I was one of the "Dam Kids," one of the children living on the River whose dad worked for Consumer's Power, operating one of the hydroelectric dams. There were very few "dam kids" when I was growing up, and none my age who lived at the Loud Dam site, my home when I first moved to the AuSable River.

The only child of Donald W. and Helen M. Weinberg, I moved with my parents from Flint, Michigan in 1942. We moved to a man's dream place, a paradise with hunting, trees, and fishing. This paradise created big problems for women. Aside from work at home, there was nothing for women to do; money was tight, and driving distances were long and difficult. During WWII, sugar and gas were rationed; we had to use stamps to get them, and the long distances between people and towns meant conserving on gas. We didn't go anywhere very often.

My story is full of events that may shock or amaze you. It's about the survival of a lonesome, only child who grew up in a very isolated area, her experiences through grade and high school. I left for a short period to work at Michigan Bell in Saginaw Michigan, returned after marrying my high school sweetheart, have lived and farmed in the area since.

I hope my love for the AuSable River comes through these stories also in my writing of this memoir of my early life.

CHAPTER 1: MEMORIES

On a bright and sunny spring day, my husband, Robert (Bob) Emerick, and I decided to go for a drive, leaving our farm of 61 years, for a short trip through the area. Little did we know what was going to happen because of this drive. We didn't have a particular direction in mind, but at the corner of F-41, we decided to go south, toward Oscoda, Michigan. As we drove, we talked of years gone by and when we started to see the changes over the years.

The town of Oscoda had grown to the north a lot with Rite Aid, Burger King where Tony Decker's used to be, Family Fare plus many smaller stores and service stores. The road is wider in places to improve the flow of traffic thru Oscoda both south and northbound in the summer because of tourism during the spring, summer and fall months. They even come in the winter for snow machine riding.

When we got near Oscoda, we passed the area where the boys had played football, but the football field was gone, all of it: the stands, the lines, the football players, the band, and the people. My first kiss had happened behind those bleachers when Bob and I started to date. I was sixteen. I had stayed with my good friend Paula Rohrer until band time then caught a ride home with Bob after our date. It was hard for us to date, as you will see later.

"Do you want to visit the dams?" Bob asked, as we stopped for the red light at the corner of US-23 and River Road in the center of Oscoda.

"Yes!" I replied, looking forward to revisiting more of our past.

As Bob turned toward the dams, I suddenly imagined a young teenaged girl standing, waiting on the road, at the back of the band. Looking harder, I saw me, dressed in my band uniform as were all the others in the band. I remembered the uniforms, blue and white, our school colors, with white stripes down the legs. We had white gloves and blue hats with white leather chin straps and a white feather plume on top. The white spats made white suede shoes look like white boots. I thought I looked smart and proud, as I held my clarinet, waiting for the majorette to give us the whistle to start our practice song.

Leading us were our two flags, the American flag and the Michigan flag. Our flags would catch the wind and fly high and proud. The majorette came next, then the band: brass in front, woodwinds in the back. Alongside, was our band director, David Merkel. He always walked along the side of the band, never inside of the band, and in full dress only. His uniform was all white in the same style as ours. Crowds of people would be looking to see what was coming next, and our flag carriers would make the people step back to give us room. Somehow, we always got through the crowds.

At that time, Oscoda had an active Air Force base located north of Oscoda. At school, the kids all called it Oscoda Air Force Base but actually the history is as follows:

1923 – 1924	Known as Loud – Reames Field
1925	Camp Skeel
1942	Oscoda Army Field
1948	Oscoda Air Force Base
1953 – 1993	Wurtsmith Air Force Base
1993	Decommissioned and closed

In 1993, after closing, the former Wurtsmith Air Force Base was turned over to a group under the City of Oscoda to care for and sell off the properties. The land was sold to private land owners or rented out. Alpena Alcona Health Center, Oscoda Area Chiropractic, Alpena Community College, a plane repair facility and many other things are now located there.

Many people would come off the Airforce base to hear us play in the band and bring their families, if they had them. Adding in the Oscoda locals made even greater crowds. We would play mostly military songs and John Phillip Sousa music. The people loved it. Even today, I look for school bands when I see a parade; a parade without a band loses a lot. We need to have children who love to play, blowing their hearts out for their country, states, schools, and for their families waiting in the crowds.

Every time we marched down Oscoda Street, the city would shut down River Road from US-23 to the first cross street. It was a safety factor; we did not have to worry about getting hit by a car while waiting on the street. This always gave me a special feeling, knowing that so many people were looking forward to hearing us play and some were watching out just for us.

Continuing down the road toward the dams, Bob and I reached the south end of our old school. Bob parked in the same area where my bus used to sit every night after school. I remember those days well. My bus was on the south side, and Bob's had always been parked at the north end of the school. Bob would walk me to my bus, until he almost missed his one time, and we decided that was not a good idea.

I have many wonderful memories from my time in that school, but today Oscoda High School "Downtown" looked lost and sad. No one was keeping up the building or the grounds. She looked like her life was coming to an end, cement cracked, glass windows broken, paint chipped, landscape either not done or ripped out and gone. Our old playground, which I had loved, is a car parking lot now.

We soon came to a small village of cabins, called Foote Site, and a little store called the DAM STORE. It is still there but seemed larger than when I was on the bus. Going on west on River Road, Bob and I came to the

AuSable River Queen, a small replica of a river boat complete with paddle wheel. The boat wasn't here when I rode the bus to school. Today, buy a ticket, and you can take a tour ride up the River.

Next to the boat launch is Oscoda Township Park. The park wasn't here in my early days either. Over the years the park has been improved and includes a nice bathroom from what we had years ago. It has a boat launch and offers a wonderful place to leave a truck and boat, by permit only. Permits can be picked up at the Oscoda Township building, the brick building at the end of River Road. That building was a library years ago when I was growing up. Years ago, this park was a nice place for dropping a boat off from your truck or trailer, and, at that time, cost nothing. We would find an empty spot between trees to park the truck until we got back. Having no dock, we waded out onto a sandy beach until soaked to the knees or higher pulling the boat out of the shallow water to deeper water and then started the motor. On cool days, your teeth would chatter while you fished.

Old Orchard Park is just about a mile west on river road from the Township Park. This park did not have very many campsites that were modern when I was growing up. They did not have inside toilets with running hot or cold water, or any camper hook-ups. In my day, there were only tent sites, outdoor toilets, and we had to pump our own water using a hand pump. Today, this park has expanded a lot as they bought more land along the river.

From Old Orchard Park going west, we saw a lot of woods with one- and two-track roads coming onto River Road. New tracks have been blazed because of lumbering and to put out forest fires. Bob and I talked about driving into Cooke Dam, but decided not to. We had already spent quite a lot of time on the road, and we needed to continue on. Talking about Cooke Dam reminded me of a friend Roberta Lacy, a bus-riding friend who was a year ahead of me in school. Roberta lived in Sid Town, about halfway in to the Cooke Dam site. She and I would sit together and talk about what we did, boys of course, and school. We always had a laugh or two. After school, we lost track of each other. My life was tied down with farming.

Soon, we arrived at Lumbermen's Monument. Over the years, the Forest Service changed the way into the area. We used to drive past the parking area on River Road, close to the Monument. The Forest Service's brochure had some interesting information about the Monument. [1]

Driving into the Monument, we decided to take a walk up to see it. Afterwards, we walked to the railing to view the AuSable. While standing there, the following memories came to both of us. A white cross stands on a hill to the right of the monument but most people do not know it is there. To find it, one must go on a long walk.

The story of the white cross happened before the dams and during the logging era. A logger died while working on the river below. His buddies carried him up the hill, buried him there, and, later, returned to place the cross at his burial site. I showed Bob where this cross was once. We made a mistake by crossing the sandy part of the hill on an angle to save time going up to the top. We tried to make a visual line from where we were to a point on the other side of the hill. The shifting sand was not stable so it

---

[1] See page 202 for information taken directly from that brochure.

moved downward when you walked on it. The line was hard to stay on and took a long time to cross! At that time, we were in good shape for walking but, at one point, thought we would not get there. We should have stayed on the solid ground and walked around the top. It was great seeing another piece of the AuSable history during the logging era.

To the west, River Road comes to an end and joins Monument Road. As Bob and I continued on Monument Rd, we turned right, going west toward M-65 and Hale or Glennie. If we had turned left, we would have ended up in East Tawas or Tawas City. A short way up the road, and along a high bank, is a memorial to people who have canoed the AuSable River. This memorial was placed by Jerry Curley's family after he lost his life in Lake Huron while practicing for the annual AuSable canoe race, which runs from Grayling to Oscoda every year. Jerry was an older Oscoda High student while I was going to school. I remember watching him in one of his races, as he and his canoe partner flew by on the river below the bank in front our house.

Driving down the road, I noticed how nice the ride felt on this hard-surfaced pavement with the smooth curves. In my day, we had had sandy gravel, dusty rough roads to navigate, and some of the curves were sharper.

The next place we came up on was Largo Springs, a great place to see if you are younger. When I was young, there were no steps, so going down to the Springs was a hard walk or slide. That area of the Springs was full of dead trees, so it was hard to actually see the Springs. By the time the steps came, I was too old to make it down and back. I saw a picture of the Springs and it looks like someone did a great job cleaning up down there.

Just a few more miles on, the road joins M-65, and we turned right toward Five Channels Dam. The road to Loud Dam, where I lived, comes off the hill on the left and goes in about 2.5 miles to the Dam. I realized that something had sure changed here. M-65 had been moved over east and the hill was lower than it had been in my day. We made a sharp left turn and were directly on Loud Dam Road. In my day, we had to come out from Loud Dam road right onto M65. My school bus had to drive down to the housing area of Five Channels Dam, go as fast as possible in the lower area to build enough speed to climb the hill for the bus in the winter. Our school bus barely made it some days but with a car, and a hard right, we usually made it. There was a barrel with sand in it at the top for those who needed sand under their tires to get enough traction on ice to make it up the hill.

In the winter, we had to miss a lot of school because of ice and snow. During a spring or two, we had wash-outs on Loud Dam Road. It took over a week to repair one of them. I was too young to walk out. Our neighbors did, but they were older. I just had a "vacation" from school, which I found boring. I wanted to go to school.

When Bob turned up Loud Dam Road, I asked him whether we really wanted to take our new car over the sand and gravel. I reminded him that cars were built higher back then; now they are "low-riders." Surprise again! The road had a hard-surface or gravel, but no sand. Even the narrow curves that I remembered were now built to allow two cars to pass each other, and there weren't any holes. The road was kept up better.

The small cabins that I remembered from my day were mostly gone; many re-sided, added onto, ripped out or replaced with homes of various sizes. Some of the vacant areas now had homes. I no longer saw the small summer cabins or hunting shacks from my days on the River. I remembered riding my bike until deer season down this road. How quiet the woods were then, with only the wind singing songs in the trees and trees cracking to the songs.

I remembered that smells were different in the spring and in the fall, even winter had a smell to it. No one wintered here in my day except the Loud Dam operators, their families, and Ox Yoke, a very small resort for fishing, hunting, run by Mr. and Mrs. Walls and their boys. Our bus picked the boys up for school. Later in the 1950s, a few people would spend the summer months on the road but come fall, they were on their way south or west for a warmer winter climate.

Bob and I finally came to the tip of the hill, a short way from the houses where I and my parents lived. On this part of the road, there are funny curves, which have been improved over the years. In the middle of the hill is a left-hand curve, and coming down the hill, there was a high hill on the left with a very wet and low swamp to the right. The last part of the road went down the hill straight. This was a great place to sled as a child. Cars were going much slower in the sand and gravel then, and there weren't many of them, so sledding was safe. Today, it would be a bad place to try sledding. Besides, back then, we could hear cars from a long way away. Cars run more quietly now, too.

As Bob and I rounded the middle curve, I could see the place where I wiped out on my bike while riding down that hill. I had ridden my bike up, almost to the top of the hill, pushed it the rest of the way, and would come back down. I had done this safely many times. That day I started wondering how fast I could go if I started back from the top, went as fast as I could to pick up speed before riding down. I thought that might be fun! I tried it, and all was fine until the curve. Perhaps, I didn't turn correctly for the left-hand curve or maybe I got into the sand on the side of the track. I will never know. However, I flew forward between the handle bars, and took a dive through sand and gravel face down. I knocked the wind out of myself and bent my bike tire. I had cuts and bruises everywhere from A to Z. Only my backside was spared. My pride was gone too, as I pushed and walked my bike home with a very sore body and bloody knees. I still carry the scars from that ride!

I remembered an angle-iron tower, too, and was excited to see the area where it used to be. I had been caught by a neighbor trying to climb it. He told me that the electric power in the lines was known to arc, so it was too dangerous to play on the towers. "Do not do it again," he scolded, and the way he said it, convinced me. I never did. The tower was on his part of the property anyway. As we approached the area, I was surprised to see that the tower was still there. Somehow it now looked smaller and shorter than when I had tried to climb it.

At the bottom of that hill was the driveway toward the Loud Dam houses. We had intended to drive in and check out the houses, but there was a "keep out" and "private" sign there. I was looking for my house, the middle, green and white one, but someone had changed the color. In fact, none of the three houses looked the same as I remembered. Some of the trees that had sung me to sleep were missing as well. The place had changed so much, all I could do was stare and remember.

I recalled our girls' p-j parties when we were in junior and senior high school and the fun we had. We talked about what we were going to do with our lives, who we liked and didn't, and why. Our talk continued through the night. Those girls still talk about how much fun they had at our house. If they had only known how much fun I had! I had finally found friends.

I remembered that the houses had looked great back then, standing proudly along the mighty AuSable, with families in them all. Shortly after I left home, my folks moved to Glennie, where they took care of a farm for a man from Detroit. They continued to live there about ten more years and then moved to Mikado, Michigan where they were closer to Bob and me.

As Bob and I sat in the car at the gate, memories flooded through me. Looking at that "keep out" sign, I knew I would have to write those memories down, for my family, my friends and for Mom and Dad, as they were a big part of my story.

Unable to get to the houses, Bob backed out to the main road and turned toward the dam itself. When I was young, we could walk across the top, or "roof," of the dam to get to the other side of the River. People would often walk up to the dam's door and ask my dad questions about the area. Dad loved to help them. He even saved a boy who almost fell into the fast-moving water of the race in front of the dam. People can't go near the dam now; "keep out" signs are all over the area. The back waters area of the dam has also been improved. Logs have been pulled out and sand brought in to create a beach area. It is easier to get a small boat or canoe in and out now. It looks nice. This whole area was much more rugged and more open when I was young. I think I had more freedom then getting around the dam area than today.

  On the way home, Bob and I talked about a lot of things and times from the past. It had been a lovely day and a lovely time for memories. Now, I had to write the story of how and why I got to that spot on the River in the first place.

CHAPTER 2: FLINT AND FAMILY

My first memories start in Flint, Michigan. I was born October 18, 1938 to Donald and Helen Weinberg. Some of my earliest memories are short, very vague, and some are stories Mom and Dad told me. I remember that our house was on Kentucky Avenue in Flint, and that it was small, with a sidewalk in front but no garage. I think the house was brown then. We lived in that house until 1942.

I remember Dad coughing a lot at night, and some days endlessly. Dad was always tired from lack of sleep. I used to sit on the floor playing with my toys and watching him try to rest in his chair between cough attacks. Nothing seemed to help. He had a bad case of asthma.

Dad worked for General Motors, in the foundry. Mom worked, too. She was a waitress in a tavern on Dort Highway in Flint before I was born. Back then, salesmen would come to the tavern to eat and drink. Women and children never went out to eat, only men. She made good money and tips until the Great Depression hit, and she got laid off. Later, Mom got a job at General Motors where she met Dad, while walking in during a shift change. She and Dad were soon laid off again because of the Depression. They got married and worked odd jobs. Between saving money from their jobs and borrowing five hundred dollars from Aunt Bertha, Dad's sister, they finally had enough money to put a down-payment on 40 acres close to Gladwin, Michigan. There was a small one room house on the property, and they lived up there for a year, until they found out I would be coming in fall 1938.

The Gladwin house was a one-room shack, with a small attic – no standing up in there – an outdoor toilet, no running water except for a flowing well in the yard. The roof and sides had light grey shingles, and there was a small barn, with the same shingles. I remember these details very well because we would go there on vacation while I was growing up.

In the summer of 1938, Mom and Dad moved back to Flint to live with Aunt Bertha. Aunt Bertha, Dad's sister, was a special person in our family. After Dad's mother died, when Dad was twelve, Grandpa and Dad moved in with Aunt Bertha. During the Depression, many people lived with one another to make ends meet. Grandpa and

Dad were still living with Aunt Bertha when Grandpa died five years later. Dad was seventeen. Aunt Bertha took care of Dad through those years and became more of a mother to him and a Grandma to me.

Mom and Dad lived with Aunt Bertha until I was one, when they moved to the small house on Kentucky Avenue. Dad got his old job back in the foundry and Mom went back to doing press work, both at General Motors. Dad worked nights, Mom worked days, and I went to nursery school. Mom would drop me off in the morning and pick me up after work. At school, we had painting classes, picked out pictures to color, and talked about what we did. I remember sleeping in the afternoons. I learned my numbers to 20, knew the alphabet, and could sing the alphabet song without a miss.

We had a dog named Dutchie. She was an older dog, and she was really Dad's dog. She wanted to go everywhere with him, including hunting. She was a good bird dog, but she wanted nothing to do with me.

While living in Flint, I remember getting the measles. Those days were awful for me. I had to stay in a dark room. Dad's room was the darkest in the house. He had long shades on the windows, as he worked nights and needed to sleep during the day. So, with the measles, that's where I stayed. They pushed the bed up against the wall. I was between Dad and the wall. My "front" was the wall, and the back was the bed's tall-foot board. I was trapped, so there I stayed, played, colored, and napped, while Dad tried to sleep. I was in diapers, so that problem was solved. I had to stay like this because measles could cause blindness. Staying in a dark room protected my eyes. I couldn't go to nursery school either, so Mom and Dad did the best they could. I had to stay in a dark room for a whole week, until the rashes were gone. That week was a hard one for all of us. The vaccine came later, so we no longer have to endure the measles any more.

Right around the time I was three, my folks and the nursery school became concerned that I was not talking. I would point to things, or I would walk quietly over to what I wanted and pick it up myself. Mom and Dad decided they would take me to a doctor to see why. During that time, I remember my father soaking his feet in a dishpan of water. I'm sure there was something in it to relieve pain, but to me it just looked like plain water. I walked up and looked into the pan. Then, I looked up at Dad and, all at once, said, "Poor Daddy's toe hoits?" My father just leaned back and laughed and laughed. I felt better because he felt better. I knew nothing about doctor appointments, but they cancelled my appointment right away. My first words included my first full sentence, plus my first question, all at once.

About a year later, after my measles episode, I was put in the back seat of our car along with Dutchie the dog. I sensed that something was different because Dutchie was put there, too. Dutchie usually had to stay home when we went anywhere together. When we pulled away from the house, Mom told me that we were going to a different place to live. Looking back through the rear window, I saw a small trailer full of our furniture. Yes, to do this, I had to stand on the car's back seat. Dutchie was laying on the seat, too, so I could only move around her. We had no seat belts, no child-protection seats; those hadn't been put in cars yet or made into laws. I'm not sure, but they may not even have been thought of yet.

We were going "up north" on US Hwy-23, much of which was gravel and sand at the time, with ruts and pot holes. It was a very bumpy, dusty road, and a long, slow trip hauling the trailer with those road conditions. After a while, I got very bored, so Mom and Dad did what many parents do: we sang the ABC song, many times, while Dad drove. I also could sit in the back area on the floor coloring in my books. Doing something helped make time go faster, but I kept thinking to myself: *How far away is this new place? It must be in a different world!*

Mom had packed a picnic basket lunch, as no one went to restaurants then. Times were still hard. Food was very expensive, and restaurants were few and far between. People were still having a hard time finding jobs. We finally stopped to take a break at a roadside park. It had only one picnic table and a trash can, nothing else. The road into the park was a circle drive, which Dad was happy about that since he was hauling the trailer behind. There were small parks here and there along the roads then, but other parks had straight drives, so Dad would have had to back up onto the grass to turn around. There were no restrooms or water for us to use. Mom always carried a pail for us women to use. I was having fun running around, until Mom told me not to do that. Dogs had been in the area and left deposits all over the place. That was hard to clean up with no extra water, so fun time stopped. Today's parks are so different!

As we drove and drove, houses were getting farther apart except in the small villages we went through. It seemed like in between there was nothing but trees and open fields. I started to notice differences in the trees. Some were larger, some smaller, some had needles and some with leaves. The air smelled different, too. We had passed many different places, finally arriving at a town called Hale. Dad said it was the last town before our new home. Finally, Dad turned into a small, narrow road, and I kept looking for a house. Mom and Dad would tell me, "not this one, not that one," until Dad turned on to a small side road. I saw three huge houses all in a line. The houses all looked alike. I wondered which one was ours. Dad went past the first one, so I knew that wasn't that one, and stopped at the second.

"This is it," Dad said.

Mom said the same, "Janice, we are here at our new home."

This was it, and we were in the middle house. I looked around; there wasn't any river that I could see. Mom had told me on the drive north that there would be a river, called The AuSable, by the house. She had also warned that I would have to be very careful because the waters were very fast and swift at times.

"You said the AuSable River is by the house. Where is it?" I asked.

"It's in the front of the house," Mom replied. "We are parked in back of the house. Dad will be working right down the road from here, at a place called Loud Dam."

Our house was on a high bank so we had to walk to the bank to see the River. Across the River, the land was lower. Wild life was everywhere: deer, bear, otter, beaver, muskrat, squirrels, bobcats, partridge, raccoons, skunks, porcupines, and snakes of many kinds, as I would gradually find out.

As I stared through the car window, I could see trees but no other people. It all seemed very strange. *Why did we have to leave where we were*? I already missed Flint, with my little house, my school, and our family. Oh, yes, then I remembered that they had been talking about trying a new way of life by moving north for Dad's health.

CHAPTER 3: OUR COMPANY HOUSE

Mom, Dad, and I got out of the car and walked to our new house. We wanted to inspect the house that was to be our new home. Compared to our Flint house, this one looked big, and I was anxious to see what the inside looked like. I wanted to see where I could play in it. The three of us walked through the rooms, which were bare, as all we owned was still in the trailer.

The house faced "backwards." The front rooms faced the River, while the back of the house was where we drove in and could enter into the kitchen. The house had two porches, one in front, toward the River, and one in back. The front porch went all the way across the width of the house. The porch was open (no screens) with pillars under a cement slab, which was the floor. Under the porch could be a good place for storing long items like oars, rakes, and lumber. We never actually used that space because snakes crawled in there, too. It harbored dozens of mosquitoes in the spring.

On the north end of the front porch was our front door, leading into a large front room that, like the porch, went across the front width of the house. On the opposite side of the front room was a stairway going to the upper floor. At the foot of the stairs was a closet. To the side of the room, on the north side was a small hallway that led back to the kitchen and to the door for the basement. On the side toward the dam, or the southwest side of the house, there was a fireplace between two windows in the living room. The back of the house on the road side was the east side of the house. The front of the house faced west.

The kitchen had a door to the back porch and there a swinging door between the kitchen and the formal dining room. The kitchen had room for a stove and refrigerator and L-shaped cupboards along two walls leading to a large sink. We had a small kitchen table to put in, and that worked fine for the three of us. In fact, this book is being written at that same table. Mom and Dad bought the stove and refrigerator after we moved in.

Through the swinging door, we came to the formal dining room. Later, we put a formal dining table in there, with folding sides and extra leaves, and had chairs to match. It could seat sixteen! There was a wooden phone on the wall with a bell-shaped bottom to talk into, and another one for your ear on the side of rectangle style phone. We had to stand in order to both talk and listen because the phone cords were very short. Through the years, this room gained a piano and a gun cabinet.

Going up the stairs, we came to an open area with six doors: one for each of the four bedrooms, access to the attic, and a full bathroom. The bathroom had a deep, claw-foot tub with a curved back. In the attic, I found that the stairs ended over the middle of the house, and there was a small open area where I could stand up without hitting my head. The roof sloped steeply down to the floor on all four sides. I picked that middle area for me to play in. That didn't last very long. It turned out to be icy cold in the winter and too hot in the summer. It had a lot of flies that Mom was forever sweeping up in the summer and fall. So, mostly I played in my bedroom or on the front porch, and outside.

The basement was the same width and length as the house, without the porches, but it was divided into smaller areas. Dad put a small workshop at the foot of the basement stairs, and there was an open wall area along the stairway that led to the pump room, which was actually under an outside cement slab. This was so that if the company (Consumers) needed to service the water pump while we were away, they could. It was heavy slab with an outside ring on it, so that the men could get into the pump room area.

Another small room was the "fruit room," which Mom would fill with things she canned as well as extra food. Mom usually shopped for a month's worth of supplies and used this area to store extras, bringing them upstairs as she needed them. Flour and sugar were stored in large cans to keep the mice out.

There was also a "utility" room with wash vats that were cement and very large and deep. The room had two clothes lines for hanging clothes to dry in the winter. Those vats became especially useful later when Mom was raising and butchering chickens to sell and eat.

The last room in the basement had a large wood and coal burner in it, along with space for wood and coal storage. We called this "the furnace room." For the winter, Dad would order how much coal he wanted, and it would be delivered to the house. The driver would open a window, put in a chute, and shovel the coal from the truck. Gravity would take the coal down the chute into the basement room, making a pile of coal.

Our house had a pump house that housed the water pump for all three Loud Dam houses at the time. The pump ran a lot, and if anyone had their water quit, Consumers Power sent a man out to fix the problem.

Later, when I was a teenager, a crew came around and added windows and screens to each of the house's front porches. This made the porch space feel more like another room of the house. We put a rocking chair, and old couch, and a small table for puzzles, and a hand-crank record player out there. It was fun to be out there, and was a good sitting or reading room almost year-round.

Dad would smoke his cigars and pipes with the window open and drink his coffee out on the porch. I put many puzzles together there, worked on scrap books, did home work, and I read every kind of book, from comic books to library books, out there.

Mom got me into books early because she read a lot. Joanne Gido, one of my cousins and I traded comic books whenever we got together. She was younger than I was, and the daughter of one of my mother's sisters, Aunt Kay

Gido. Distance was a great factor and gas rationing really made going to Flint impossible for a while.

The back porch was small, but useful. It was a place to hang coats and boots, and we kept tools like pails, mops, rakes, shovels, hand saws, etc., there. It also gave us a place to keep salt for melting ice in the winter.

All the dam houses looked the same: dark green second story, dark shingles on the roof, a white first story, with white trim on the window and corners. With some minor differences, most of the inside layout was basically the same. The differences were in the inside colors. All of these Aladdin homes were shipped from Sears and Roebuck in pieces and built on site for Consumers Power.

As these were company houses, Consumers decided the colors inside the houses. The company ordered the paint needed according to how many bedrooms, kitchens, front rooms, etc. Crews worked on one house, then went to the next, until each house at every dam was re-painted. This took several years, and houses were re-painted about every ten years. If the renter really did not like the color offered when the crews came, the renter could exchange for paint left over from other jobs. Renters could also buy their own paint and paint the rooms themselves, but Consumer's would not reimburse. Mom always said "why bother. Let them paint." I only remember her changing colors once, for my bedroom. The color that year was green. Oscoda school colors were blue and white, and that's what I wanted, and got.

CHAPTER 4: DAMS

With a 2800-foot wall, Loud Dam was one of six dams built on the AuSable River to produce electricity. Loud Dam was built in 1913. This was the beginning of electricity being made available to rural areas of Michigan. A lot of people in the area waited a long time to get the lines in to service them. We always had power from the time we came to live in the company house.

The machinery for building the dams was brought down to the power house for shipping out. Everything needed was shipped in from Oscoda on a Railroad spur; materials from Alcona and Mio were brought in by trucks and horses. Cement was sent in by railroad cars and gravel was taken out of the gravel pit, which was at the top of a hill at the backwater of Loud Dam.

The working organization at the Loud development consisted of approximately 400 men. Most of them lived with their families at the site while building the dams. At the time there were over 100 children. Dan McQuaigs general store supplied practically everything the families needed. This small community of workers meant a lot of business for the store. (Alcona Country Review 5-22-1913).

Investors had hoped that the land around the dams would sell and draw in new residents. When the dams were finished, the area didn't grow in population as hoped. Eventually, housing for the initial families and crews were torn down. (*Alcona County Herald,* 6-26-1914).

Wandering and exploring the area as a child, I remember finding some old foundations scattered here and there on the hill at the backwater of Loud Dam. I think those might have been where the workers lived while building the dam. There was also a gravel pit those workers dug using the nearby resources to build the dam. At one time, a school was there, too, but it was gone by the time I moved in. I started kindergarten after we moved when I was four. I turned five in October.

Today, there is a sign to not enter the gravel pit area. Consumer's has high tension towers going up the hill now and built a substation between the dam and the hill. This substation serves more people and uses another line to carry electricity to a high-tension line high above. When

I was growing up, those high tension towers were not there. There was a railroad track into the gravel pit where I saw rattlesnakes. I will bet there are rattlesnakes still up there, sunning themselves on a warm spring or summer day. This was not a good place to visit.

My dad was assigned to work at Loud Dam as an operator. At that time, it took men working in shifts to run the dams. There was always a man on site at each dam day and night. They had to report every hour to Saginaw. Each dam had four assigned operators; one man was the "supervisor" for all of the dams. The supervisor handled work when men called in sick or needed to be absent, or if there was any trouble. Whatever an operator had trouble with went to and through the supervisor. He lived in a house at Five Channels Dam; his house was like ours but off by itself, across the road from the operators' home. The supervisor also checked each dam regularly to make sure that the operators were doing things correctly.

The men working different shifts put limits on our lives. Children had to be quiet and do things quietly. There were three shifts each day. One man worked 8:00 a.m. to 4:00 p.m.; one worked 4:00 p.m. to 12:00 a.m.

(midnight); the third worked from 12:00 a.m. (midnight) to 8:00 a.m. At the end of this rotation, they got a couple of days off. Then, the shifts started all over again. People never knew who was working or who was sleeping. I really had to play quietly inside, too, when Dad was sleeping. It was hard to do but became a way of life in the end. There was a fourth operator who lived Hale and drove to the dam for every shift he had. He covered vacation days, sick days, and time off for the other three operators. The shifts always started over the same way month after month. Each operator had cleaning duties while working. There was a board somewhere that told the men what each one needed to do during their shift. For example, they had to make sure windows were shut, general maintenance, watch people fishing and running around in the front of the dam. If the men saw something dangerous outside, they asked the people to stop.

The only part of the dam that was heated back then was the small room closed off from the generators. This was to protect the men from the noise the generators made. In the winter the room was cold because every dam was open to the roof and all the heat went up. The floor area was always cold in the winters. In this room, the men had a space heater they could run when needed. All the switches the men used were on this inside wall, so they could tell how the dam was working. The operators reported dam conditions to the office in Saginaw every hour. The Saginaw personnel knew all the levels from each of the dams down the river. It was very important to monitor water levels of the each dam to prevent a dam washout from high water pressure. The operator would spill on Saginaw's say so one by one down the river.

A spill is a controlled release of water pressure from the backside of the dam and released through a spill gate. The spill does not run through the dam. It runs a long side of the dam and is located outside the area of the generators to the side of the dam buildings. Dams usually continue running while spilling water off the side. This is so that the water won't get over a level mark above the dam. Too much water creates too much pressure and could take the dam out. This is why dams are monitored closely.

As the AuSable runs from Grayling to Oscoda, it serves a very large watershed. Somewhere up the River, it might be pouring rain, while another might be in sunshine. Water levels were reported to Consumer's headquarters in Saginaw hourly; Saginaw sent back an order to each dam operator to spill when the water level rose. How much water spill to be removed depended on whether one or two spill gates had to be switched on.

One year, lightning hit a line or tower and ran down the line to Loud Dam. It tripped a switch. A line man looked at it and replaced an insulator or two. The dam operator was told when to switch that line back on – a quick fix.

In another incident, a line was hit by lightning. The lightning burned and melted a switch right out of the wall. Mr. Heine was working at the time and was trapped by the fire that had started. Thankfully, he was able to get through the back door of the switch room. There was fire burning in the panel inside the room. On the other side, molten metal was running across the floor toward the generators. Mr. Heine was finally able to reach the stairway to the top of the dam. He then ran across the top and back down the outside stairway, around and back into the dam where he was able to put the fire out, finally reporting to Saginaw. Outside, the emergency horns were blaring, telling everyone that there was trouble at Loud Dam.

Each dam had its own emergency horns, which could be heard at the houses, so that men could go to help. Dad went down to help but it was all under control when he arrived. Consumers sent a lot of people out to repair this one. They cleaned, repaired and painted, and everything went back to normal. They move fast so that lights can come back on for us to use. These men go in the worst conditions to fix hot wires in wet conditions. Remember that when your power goes out!

SAFETY ON THE DAM

Dad loved to visit and I would see him talking to fishermen on the River. He must have answered a million questions that people asked about the dams. He also watched for dangerous things and stopped them before things got out of control. Most people were good about doing what he told them. Consumers Power always stressed safety first. The men were trained to follow specific safety rules, and they all enforced them. Mom and Dad taught me early on what I could and could not do so I knew when Dad was going to say "Stop!" This meant no running, no sitting with feet over the wall, and no sticking a head through rails or bars. I had learned quite a few lessons in handling people through him.

RIVER WATER AND DAMS

The AuSable River can be very dangerous because of the moving water from the dams. We used to fish below Five Channels Dam in a "bay" of the River. In winter, that "bay" froze very hard and was considered a safe place. If fishing behind a dam, people have stay away from the Triangular poles behind it. These poles are placed into a triangular formation on the backside of the dam to prevent blockage on the dam grates from debris such as logs, trash, etc. Water going through the dam creates a pull. This pull is so strong it can pull big logs into the dam grates, which must be cleaned now and then.

One year, Consumer's Power brought in a deep-sea diver to clean the grates out. He had the twist-on-air helmet type suit with weights on his feet to keep him submerged. He put chains on each of the logs and the crew lifted them out with a winch. This would allow more water to pass through the dam and out the front. I liked watching him get his gear on, which wasn't a fast job. Everything had to be screwed on. It took two other people just to get him dressed. He could only work for two hours underwater to avoid the bends. They came back to do it all again the next day. I could see his air bubbles come up from down below was fun but also scary. His life depended on the generator (a small one) to pump air down to him. At that time, I could watch him work, and I'm glad I had that opportunity. Today, our laws would not allow people to get that close to the dam.

Growing up as a child of a dam operator, I learned the dangers and safety precautions necessary to cross over the top of the dam. I would walk down three steps, walk across the roof of the dam, and pass the spill gates, up three steps onto the dike on the west side of the river. There, I picked morels and white morels, hunted deer, and took many walks to occupy my day.

One year was special, really something to watch. We had lots and lots of snow that year, followed by a very quick melt-down. It rained and rained, and soon water was gushing down places it had never run before.

All the streams, big and little, were full and overflowing, so both spill gates were opened for more than a day. The water going over would hit the cement under the dam in the River and came back up into the air.

This created a watery mist falling like rain encased in the glistening rays of a brightly shining sun. Suds formed on top of the flowing, rushing water. This sudsy water boiled down the spillways to drop into the river below, only to rise toward the sun and sky, turning over onto itself creating many rainbows in the water as it fell. Then the water raced down the river spreading out in all the low areas moving fast. The water that year went above the normal water lines and was lapping at tree trunks that were normally on dry land, but were now in the river. This happened at each dam on the River until the water reached Foote Dam where it raced with unbridled urgency toward Oscoda to spread and relax into Lake Huron.

ROADS

The roads at that time were only gravel, sand with large pot holes and ruts, especially in the spring and late fall. When it rained, the roads got very muddy. Between the Loud Dam and Ox Yoke, there was a cut off road that went through the woods to M-65. This road was used by the dam people and the summer people to save about five miles getting to Hale. It was a one-track sandy road, was prone to washout downhill in heavy rains. If two cars met, one of them would have to pull off between trees along the road. We called it "Gully Road." It all seemed to work, as people made sure everyone was out of trouble given the sandy conditions. If someone did have trouble or got stuck, one of the other drivers would stop in the road and help get the car out.

One year, "Gully Road", our one-track cut off road to Hale, which we used only from spring to fall, washed out. It filled one of the cabins' yards full of sand. I think that road is still used today, but I'm not sure. We had to take the long way to Hale for a while, and found the main road also had a deep, two-foot gully wash-out as well. I was off school for two weeks because the bus could not come in to pick me up. I would have rather gone to school.

Shortly after we moved up north, Mom placed three electric candles, one tall and two short ones on a decorative board and plugged it into a wall socket. Mom put it in the south living room window so that Dad could see it from the Dam. While this looked like a Christmas decoration, it was lit whenever Dad was working nights or afternoons year around. The bulbs had very heavy reflectors clipped to them to spread the light for Dad to see.

Years later, I asked Mom why the candle lights were on year 'round. She told me, "your father always wanted it on when he worked so that he could see where his house was in the dark. That light meant home and that his family was waiting for him. Perhaps this was an effect of losing his parents early in his life. Dad was 12 when his mother died, and 17 when his father died. After his mother passed away, Dad and his father moved in with dads' oldest sister, Bertha and her husband (Aunt Bertha and Uncle Vern). At that time, male children were taught to suck-up their feelings and move on. Some, like Dad, may have had a very hard time of it.

Dad moved out of Aunt Bertha's home when Dads' other sister Rosalie died in childbirth with her fourth child. Rosalie's husband was in poor health and couldn't raise the new baby or care for the other kids. Aunt Bertha decided that the new baby would be her adopted son. Rosalie had three other children, at the time of her death; one girl and two boys. The girl, Arlene, was married. Bob, the oldest boy, was working his way through college and later becoming a Pharmacist. Stan joined the service in World War II and flew airplanes. The new baby's father died shortly after the adoption. Dad told me this story when I asked about his family. Times were hard then. Multi-family living was a common way of life back then with some families raising other family's children.

Dad's light still shines in my window every Christmas in his memory. Everyone loved him. My children would run to him, asking for a stick of gum. He always had a pack of gum in his pocket ready for them and a quarter for each of them. He was a man of few words, but a great, great man, father and grandfather to my children.

Front Room in Flint   My first tricycle

My First Perm

Dad, his fish and me

Our house at Loud Dam

Mom Ice Skating on the backwaters of Loud Dam

Loud Dam 1960

Loud Dam today

Back Waters of Dam today

Scenic view of the River

CHAPTER 5: ON MY OWN

I was about three years old in the summer of 1942 when we moved. Everything seemed strange and bare, only woods, dirt roads, and three houses standing in a cluster, or alone on the river bank. After being in nursery school all day during the week with other children while in Flint, now I was left to find things to do on my own.

As a girl, I found it hard to live in this environment. This was a man's dream life. I wanted to live like my cousins, who were shopping, doing everything in school, and generally having fun. My doing such things was limited because of the distance to cities, shopping malls and the depression.

Dad quickly made lots of friends along the River with the men working his shift and also among the city and cottage people who came. Even after retirement he remained friends with many of them.

It was different for Mom. Mom told me that the women froze her out of things they did because Dad had gotten the job that some locals wanted. They "cliqued out" the "outside." She found her way by reading, helping Dad haul wood, crocheting, sewing and taking care of the house. She found ways to survive.

When we moved in, I learned that we had three boys as neighbors, who were older and didn't want to play with me. I had to find things to do by myself. At first, Mom and Dad told me to stay in the yard because of snakes. There was a girl, Joan Heine, who was eight years older and she baby sat me from time to time. She also taught me beginning piano lessons. There was also one boy, Carl Walls, 4 years younger, who lived up the road at Ox Yoke. None of us had anything in common because of our age differences. After having other children around in nursery school for a year and a half, I now had no one, and it got lonely. I was looking forward to going to school, but even after I started school, I was too shy and friends lived too far away for me to find playmates. I managed, but it was a lonely life for some time.

To occupy myself at home, I tried to find things to do. It was hard, especially when it rained or snowed, so I stayed in the house a lot of the time. I was never a doll person. I did like to dress paper cut out dolls, but I quickly lost interest in them. I cut pictures of models the

Sears and Roebuck catalog and different clothes to fit them, or I cut pretty scenes from outdoor magazine or cards, made scrapbooks, put puzzles together and read.

On nice warm, sunny days, summer through fall, I would go out, and play in the sand box Dad made for me. I had a few sand box toys. I made underground garages and cities with sticks for light poles and string for wire and little houses down the streets. I fenced in animals with sticks, like the old rail fences. Small stones were cows and horses. I had farms, castles that had moats with water in them. Some of these works of art turned out looking great, until it rained.

Eventually, I got a scooter, two wheels, a bar with handle for two hands, a running board to put my foot on, and painted red. I used this to zip up and down the sidewalk at the back of the house. I also had a sled, until it broke, after that we pulled out a toboggan, and I got a bicycle that I used for many years.

I found the oars for our boat and made a horse out of one. I rode it around the yard and tied it to a tree. Sometimes I would pack a lunch and eat on top of the hill by the River under a white pine tree. Dad told I would have to stop using his oars because I wore one out on the side by dragging it everywhere. I actually wanted a real horse very badly at that time. I did get to ride at a riding stable, but I really wanted the pony that I rode there. As I grew, I became too heavy for the pony, and Mom and Dad couldn't afford the upkeep of a horse.

After we settled in, a memory kept coming back to me of another child in the house playing with me. I thought that perhaps the child must have died, so I asked Mom, "Why did you only have me? Did a brother or sister die?" Mom said "no." Mom told me that she had had seven operations after I was born. The doctors found that she had a lot of infection and couldn't have more children. She told me that she had babysat for my Aunt Angie, Mom's sister, for a while. My cousin Margie McQuigg is two years older than I am, and she's the one I was missing from my life. We had left her back in Flint, and now I was stuck up north with a lot of trees. I knew it was up to me to find something to do.

One thing I liked to do was to watch the snow fall at night. With our street lights on every night because of the dam, I could lay on my bed upstairs and fall to sleep while watching snow drift lazily down, like flies moving around a light in summer. The dropping snow was beautiful to watch, and I watched all sizes and shapes of flakes waft slowly to the ground or blow by quickly in a blizzard. In the morning after a heavy snow, the pine limbs would droop toward the ground, feeling the weight of snow on their shoulders. Sometimes only the tips of the branches would be covered. Seeing the snow in the morning was nice to wake up to; it was like God had painted the trees especially for me.

Christmas was special time, even if there weren't many presents under the tree. Our Christmas tree had only a few lights, one or two lines on a 6-8-foot tree, homemade ornaments, and popcorn strung on a string, usually three strings, depending on how much we ate! Our stockings were hung from the mantle. All three, "Janice," "Mom," and "Dad," each filled with an orange, an apple, some candy, a package of gum, plus a few nuts in the shell. I was also given one gift, either a toy or some clothes. Mom and Dad never exchanged with each other. Maybe they were used to doing without a Christmas gift during the hard times of the Depression. There was never very much happening for very long under the tree on Christmas morning.

"This is Jesus's birthday," Mom always said, and then she would read the "Christmas Story" to me.

AT FIRST

The roadway from our house to the Dam was scary at night! It was my job to carry Dad's supper to the Dam for him. It was the 4 p.m. to 12 a.m. shift that got me. He liked a hot meal for supper, although other times he would carry his lunch box with sandwiches and coffee.

When it was windy out, it was even scarier. The street lights would swing back and forth causing limbs to move and make all kinds of things move on the road surface or even fly toward me. My mind would run away with imagining what was coming toward me. Sometimes there were faces without bodies or bodies without heads running at me. Cats big like tigers, snakes, bears and things flying at me like shovels, hoes and knives thrown at me by a unknown source.

It was only a half mile or so down to the Dam from the house, and less by the River. I would have to walk down around 6:00 p.m. In the summer this was fine because it was light and warm out until much later. When winter came, it was cold and dark. The street lights were spaced just right to create shadows on both sides of the light poles, shadows were created from small trees waving in the wind, high weeds, and shrubs along the road. I saw everything in those shadows that I could imagine: a "monster" family, "animal" families, etc. I remember my heart pounding, wondering if I was going to make it to the Dam and Dad. I would walk fast down the road thinking bears were watching me. I wondered, do snakes crawl at night? A child's brain can sure work overtime from fear.

In the early years, my imagination would run away with me when I walked in the woods. At first, the trees seemed scary, but I grew to love them. These tall trees towering above me became ancient mothers with arms stretching down to comfort me. As these mothers swayed in the wind, the branches became arms wrapping around me, and the wind blowing through them talked to me gently, telling me "things will get better; it won't always be like this."

ENTER SUZIE

To keep myself occupied, I went for walks. I colored in books or put puzzles together. I had scrapbooks, and I used magazines to cut and paste pictures into them. Later, I had books and the Nancy Drew series. Sometimes I played cards by myself. These were the kind of things that kept me going, along with having very good parents and a bunny named Suzie.

One day when I got off the school bus, Dad told me, "Come, see what I found today." I saw a box, and when I opened it, there was a bunny. I named it Suzie. She was all white with pink eyes and long ears. She was small and only a hand-full.

Suzie loved to eat and she grew and grew into a very large rabbit. Dad built a cage with a roofed in area at the back, so I could lift up the roof to clean. The rest of the cage was wire all around, over and under. One day, I checked on Suzie and went running back into the house.

"Mice are attacking Suzie," I yelled.

Dad went out to check and came back with a smile on his face. Everything is ok, he told us.

"She's given birth to 16 bunnies."

But, how did that happen? No one knew.

However, our neighbor had a male rabbit that got out of his cage one night. Dad wondered if it might have been a wild rabbit, too. When Suzie's babies grew up a little, there was a miniature "Peter" that looked just like the rabbit next door. Apparently, rabbits can mate through a wire cage.

When I was about ten, we took Suzie and her bunnies with us for a week's vacation at our Little House in the country. While there, some of the bunnies went wild. No matter how much we tried, we could never catch the wild ones again. We had to leave them behind. We took the biggest share of bunnies that we had captured back to the Dam house with us. Suzie, and her now reduced number of half-grown bunnies, were all females. "Peter Rabbit II" stayed behind with a few of his sisters and brothers. They were old enough to care for themselves at this time. Peter had always been wild and hated being held, so he wasn't missed much.

We sold Suzie and her bunnies to a lady who raised rabbits. We couldn't eat them; they were all friends by now. Dad said that they were eating us out of the house.

Selling them was ok with me, as I had lost interest in the rabbits by then. The baby bunnies were cute, but rabbits are only rabbits. Only Suzie was special to me. The lady who bought her used her as breeding stock.

HAIR PERMS

Because of the Shirley Temple fame, all the mothers were copying her hair style for their girls so my mother got the bug & I had to get a perm. To get a perm in the 40's, one looked like they were going to set off on a space trip at any minute. There was a pole with wires & clamps on the ends in different lengths. The hairdresser rolled your hair and then clamped one on the wires over the roll. As they went on your head they got heavier and heavier until it felt like your neck would not support the weight. The hairdresser would turn the perm machine on and you sat and sat while your hair seemed to fry as it was hot enough to do so. When they final took the clamps off and took the rollers out you felt free at last. That was the one and only for me. I told Mom I didn't care if I looked like a man but I was never going through that again! Boy was Shirley Temple hated that day. I found out much later my cousin Margie had her hair done like that first. Mom decided that look was necessary for me. Yes, because of family ties, Marge and I were almost twins. The only difference was she had brown eyes and I had blue.

CHAPTER 6: STARTING SCHOOL

At first, while I was in kindergarten, Mom would walk me out to the bus in front of the first house on our road. There she would wait with me until the bus came. I was small and it was all I could do to get on. The steps were also steep for my little legs. I remember grabbing at the top rail because the bus was already lurching forward before, I was on.

Once, when I was in kindergarten or first grade, I missed my bus going home because I had to use the bathroom after school. I walked down the hall to the bathroom then went out on the side where my bus parked. No bus. So, back into school I went, climbing up the long flight of steps going to up to the first floor from the south side. All the rooms were off the long hallway where the bathrooms were at the back. Back then, because I had short legs, climbing up and down that stairway was hard. No one was in the hallway, and I didn't know what to do.

At the other end of the hall, was a huge man, who looked up and started walking towards me. I started to cry and was scared stiff. By this time, I was sure that I would never find my Mom and Dad again. The man kept coming toward me, but he was smiling while I was bawling. He bent over me and asked me what was wrong. When I told him that my bus was gone, he asked "which one?" I didn't know the number or what the driver's name was, but I did tell the man that "it's the one that sits by itself on that side of the school."

"Oh no," the man said, "it's the River Road bus!"

"Yes," I nodded.

"Well," he said, "we will have to try to catch it. Do you have all your things to take home with you?"

"Yes", I said again.

We went out to his Packard; I got into the front seat with him, and we took off. I have never ridden as fast as I did that day on River Road! Trees and dust were flying by, but we caught up with my bus at Foote Site.

"Is this one of yours?" the man asked the driver. Hearing a "yes," the man handed me over to the driver and I was on my way home.

Life was very different then. People helped one another without a thought. This man had a child with a problem to protect and he saw to it. This man was Sutherland Hayden, the principal of the school for many years, and he was well-known by most people of that time period. Us kids always referred to him as "Sud." If a principal would do this today, there would be an uproar.

When I was in the first grade, we got a new bus driver, one that chewed tobacco. I was not aware of the chew, until he spit into a rag at my stop. I smelled the slimy mess because the heater blew warm air, and when the door opened, the smell rushed right at us. With my short legs on steep steps, I was afraid of losing my balance and falling or stepping on that spit-rag. The smell would also upset my stomach, kind of like having car sickness, for the hour-long bus ride. The good thing was that the bus driver didn't last long.

Even after I started school, it took me a long time to find friends. Living as isolated as we did, made me very shy. My school was over 20 miles away, so a friend's house was too far away for me to get to easily, and the same for a friend to come to me. I also knew that we couldn't have friends come to our house for over-nights because of Dad's work schedules. He needed to sleep. Quiet was the way of life, and gas rationing made driving anywhere difficult. Besides, there were many cliques in school. There were the local town kids, the Air Force kids, and the farm kids. The few dam kids like me were definitely out numbered. In later years, we also had kids from one-room and smaller area schools coming into the higher grades.

Eventually, I got better at overcoming the shyness problem and found friends in school. As I grew older, I made friends in each of the groups, and I felt accepted in all of the groups, but it took me a long time to leave shyness behind.

SCHOOL CLOTHES

Mom, Dad, and I always had nice clothes but we never had the number of pieces that we have today. This was just after the Depression, so money was short and gas was rationed. Mom and Dad used a lot of what they had for money and gas stamps to move from Flint. Feed for the chickens, as well as other animals, was delivered to the Hale Grain Elevator and put in cloth sacks made of cotton. When the feed was sold in small quantities, the elevator would keep the sacks. Farmers bought, kept what they needed and then had the sacks re-filled. The

Grain Elevator would have a lot of new, empty feed sacks and sell these to women for making clothes.

Mom kept her feed bags to sew things from, and she bought more. This was a cheaper way to buy the amount of material need for clothes. In those days, a lot of women did their own sewing; some even made men's suits, which takes talent. I used to think I was the only one who had to wear feed sacks for clothes. Later, a group of girls I had known were talking at a class reunion, and I found that they had worn them, too. Their mothers were sewing feed sack clothes, too, and some of them were worse off than I was and had fewer clothes and wore hand-me-downs.

Quantity of clothing was another factor. I had five outfits for school and one good one for Sundays or special occasions. My older clothes that still fit, I used for play clothes. Mom also made shorts and pants for summer for me to play in. Sometimes, hand-me-downs and older clothes were ripped apart and re-cut for a new outfit to play in, or, if new enough, to use "for good." But cotton faded quickly back then, so re-using materials for good was rare.

CHAPTER 7: WWII AND HARD TIMES

September 2, 1945 marked the end of WW II, but between our arrival in 1942 through 1945, the War was very much part of our lives. Dad was exempt from serving in the military because of his asthma and, probably, his job was a priority, given the country's need for electricity. I remember several events that happened during War time and were affected by the War.

I remember hearing talk about the War and its progress, including hearing news of the War on the radio once dad got a short-wave. I remember feeling a kind of tension that the War could come to our part of the world. We had the Air Force base in Oscoda, which was used for training, and we would hear bomber planes going over head. At one point, we had planes from the Oscoda Airbase making practice runs on the AuSable River dams. They would follow the River and dive down onto the dams to a certain height. We could see the planes flying tightly together. I found it a frightening thing to watch, and I was scared because of Dad working there. I remember one particular episode distinctly. I remember the "French Flyers."

On July 12, 1944, the Oscoda Airbase became the site of the Free French Air Force training group. One lieutenant and thirty-four enlisted flight students arrived at the base for training. This coincided with a complete transfer of personnel from Blackstone A.A.F, which started a new era of high activity at the base. Base personnel numbers more than doubled in three months. Under this set up, the 13th A.A.F base unit consisted of four sections: medical, supply, administration, and the French group. A training program was set up that consisted of subjects designed to prepare personnel for shipment to combat zones. Subjects ranged from gas warfare to first-aid and classroom instruction was supplemented by field exhibits, movies, and lectures. The French unit was in Oscoda until October 1944, during the time that they were getting trained as a combat crew. We used to watch them from the playground at school. We would see them high in the sky making circles and loops in the air, chasing each other up and down. We were all praying the war wouldn't come to us.

Four planes from the French Fliers, as we referred to them, skimmed the very tops of our Michigan white pines. I was standing in the yard by the sidewalk to the house when I heard them coming. It seemed that I heard them coming for a long time. I wondered if they were coming to bomb us. I knew this wasn't only one or two practice planes like what had passed through before. These were loud and there seemed to be a steady hum that got louder and louder. I just knew that they were coming to get us for sure. I wanted to warn Mom but was frozen to the ground. Suddenly, it was too late to do anything. There they were, coming out from under sun, flying above the trees, just missing the high wires running to Five Channels Dam and the Loud Dam.

I stood there, looking up, and the lead plane tipped its wing. They were so close to those pine trees and our house. The plane was so close I could see the pilot smile and wave his hand at me. Another man was talking to the pilot and adjusted his position so that he could see me better. I could see them all talking inside and laughing. I ran to the River and watched the Dam with my knees shaking until the planes flew on following the River. They had flown right over the Dam.

Later people were talking about what the French group did in Oscoda and AuSable area, including one plane that flew under the bridge on US -23. Someone checked out the complaint and measured; apparently there was only a three-inch clearance on each side of the plane's tips. Shortly after that the French group was shipped home to France. I'm sure that everyone breathed a sigh of relief.

Another WWII era event that really stands out for me has to do with a bat and the Air Force base in Oscoda, Michigan. When I was about 5 or 6, I was playing baseball with the boys next door. It must have been some holiday because we were all home. Mom left me to play, while she went to take dad his supper at the dam and she wanted to fish for a while.

I got too close to the batter, or he threw the bat. I know that I got hit full swing on the right side of my head. It tore my skin three-quarters of the way off, the width of the end of the bat. I remember thinking, I have to go home. I started going and then the house started tipping over. I saw it pick up speed and then it was half way over. Then, everything went dark.

When my memory came back, I was on my neighbor Mrs. Heine's counter, and she was cleaning my hair and head with clean cloths. I could see that my pretty dress was red from top to bottom in front. Mrs. Heine was very worried about me and was wrapping my head tightly trying to stop the bleeding. Mom and Dad came in on a run. They made some phone calls and decided that I needed stitching. But it was a holiday, and, at that time, there were no doctors and no hospital between us and Bay City, about 75 miles away. With all the blood loss, they didn't think I would make it. So, they called the Air Force base in Oscoda, and the base doctors said they would take me. Some of the best Air Force doctors were training at the base right then. Now, they had themselves a live patient.

The base was closed to civilians because of the War; only base personnel were allowed past the gate. I was going in and out of consciousness on our way to the base, which was 25 miles away or more. The doctors had said to keep me upright, so Mom held me all the way.

I was really bleeding. The bath towels that they had wrapped around my head were soaked when we finally got to the base. But the base was ready for us. Two military Jeeps with four men in each met us. The soldiers were in full uniform, with rifles pointed up on their knees. They were to escort us to the hospital. They got out of the Jeep and jumped to the running boards on our car: one stood by the driver, another by me on the passenger side, and one each on the back. At that time, cars had running boards running from wheel well to wheel well because they were built higher off the ground, and people had to step up to get in. Another car was right behind us with four soldiers in it. We had a full military escort, with a lot of soldiers around us, all the way to the hospital. I guess that because it was war time, the base wasn't taking any chances with this not being legitimate.

The soldiers all left once the doctor took my bandage off. The doctor used a butterfly stitch to sew up my skin. I don't remember how many stitches he put in, but there were a lot of them. He told Mom to take me to our regular doctor, Dr. Hess, in East Tawas on Monday. He wanted Dr. Hess to check for infection. The doctor also told Mom that if I started to pass out or had other signs of severe concussion, to take me to Bay City. He gave her a salve to spread over the area and told her to keep changing the bandages until the bleeding stopped. Then, he gave her some extra bandages and said we should leave, the same way we had come in. But, when we walked out the hospital door, no one else was in sight, so we drove slowly to the gate.

We didn't get another escort, but the soldiers on guard duty all waved good-by as we went through the gate. That was unusual, as they were always very serious and business-like. They must have been worried that I wasn't going to make it because of the blood all over me. Besides, they were also probably thinking about all the children, brothers and sisters they had at home. The good news for me was that after a few days the skin healed, and I was fine. I am very grateful that we had the Air Force base close by.

Even after WWII ended, we found reminders of the War's effect on our area. Mom and Dad and I would sometimes go for a drive on the fire lanes in the area. These one-track roads were on both sides of the River. Most of them were in square miles, but smaller tracks had been cut through on angles from the roads. These were to stop forest fires from moving forward. The smaller ones were fine for walking but not for driving because of the limbs and brush left along them. A car or truck would have a lot of scratches on it.

One day while on a ride a few years after WWII was over, we drove over the Five Channels bridge and were going north on M-65. We turned right off M-65 and followed a fire lane track toward the east. I was having fun. Dad would come to a cross-road and would say "left or right." I would tell him one or the other and off we would go. It was an adventure.

We came to a swampy area, and Dad thought we needed to turn around and go the other way. We didn't. We saw where lumbermen were taking wood out in the area, but their equipment was idle at the moment, so we could get through, and we continued on. We found some additional roads back somewhere that were more improved than our usual one-tracks, which surprised us a bit. Then we came to a large rectangular pit dug out in sand where they drove in and out of. It was full of shell casings, some still loaded. Maybe lumbermen or whoever was cleaning up the sites were finding practice bombs on the bombing range and maybe they found some unexploded, real bombs out there too.

Whatever they had found or trucked in was being buried in pits and covered back up with sand, somewhere back there in the woods. Wherever these shells came from, exploded or not, someone was making those disappear. Those covered pits are still there today, wherever, whether in one large pit or in many of them, who knows. Dad said that we must have crossed the line unto base property. Had we seen a sign stating "Danger, Do Not Cross this Line"? Of course, not! We had not even seen a "Keep Out" sign.

Later, Dad found a man who had found a pit, too, and had the knowledge to disarm some of the shells. Dad built a lamp from one of the shell casings that he got from this man. I still have it. It makes a nice small night light for the bedroom.

Today's Oscoda Village is on old base property. A lot of the buildings were torn out and some buildings and hangers are used for businesses now. The area where we found the pit was where the base did practice bombing flights during the War. It was all wild then. Now there are small cabins and homes scattered here and there all over that area. I wonder if the owners know about the pits.

Going on these rides now and then was a lot of fun. We saw a lot of different animals, and we used to see herds of deer. Back then, we could stop and count 100 deer in one herd. Even the small groups had 25 to 50 deer in them. Now, I'm told that it's hard to find deer on State land, and most hunters will say it's not like it was. Today, the deer have found our farm lands, winter or summer, and our crops.

CHAPTER 8: THE BIG HILL AND JESUS

I was around 8 or 9 when I started to walk to the big hill on the left side of the road coming in. I had never been up there and wondered what it looked like on top. I was feeling pretty down because there wasn't anyone to play with! So, I just started walking through the neighbor's mowed out area to the road to save time getting to the hill. Then, I walked up the road to a place on the right where I could get across the ditch. Most of that ditch was wet all the time because of springs.

Once on the other side, I started up the hill. It was loaded with all kinds of trees, pine, maple, birch, and many other kinds. The wind was blowing somewhat, just enough to make music. It was dark because there were so many trees and the leaves and bushes were thick. As I walked, and in some places crawled to get up the hill, I wished that I had another girl my age to do things with and to talk to, and most of all to share my walks through the woods. This was what I would call a "poor Janice day."

It took some time to get up that hill. It was a hard climb, at least where I was, and I never went that way again. This day was when I learned to walk on an angle to the hill in a zig-zag pattern, back and forth, to reach the top. When I finally reached the top, looking around me, I found the remains of an old foundation, rectangular, in shape, with cement steps toward the hill.

Half way up the hill, I had been thinking that maybe I should just quit and go back. I started to remember something about Jesus. I had heard this in one of the many different churches we had gone to while I was growing up. Mom was raised a Catholic and Dad was Methodist, so they went to different churches trying to find one they could belong to. What I remembered was the song, "What a friend I have in Jesus". Thinking about that song, I kept talking to Jesus on the way up. I believe that he was leading me to this spot on the hill.

At the top of the hill, I asked Jesus, if he would be my friend and guide me all my days. I told him that I did not have any friends to play with and asked if he would walk, talk with me and be my friend forever. By then, I was kneeling on the steps of that foundation. I asked Jesus to help me find the right church to join because they were all different and had different rules. How would I know the right one to choose?

"Jesus," I said again, "if you will be my friend, I will always have you with me wherever I go. And, "Jesus, someday when I'm older, would you find a lonesome boy for me to marry? If you do, he and I would understand each other and have a happy marriage." Lastly, I thanked him for my good parents.

As I stood up, I knew that Jesus had heard my prayer. I knew he would be leading me, healing me, and walking with me through life's ups and downs. I knew that I would find great friends someday. I knew then that I had a friend forever, and I would be okay.

This was the area where the workers and their families lived while building the dam. I have always carried the love I found that day with me where ever I go. I have never gone back because it was so hard to get up the hill in that area. I know my friend is with me no matter what happens. He has watched over me in many ways over the years.

CHAPTER 9: THE WOODS

We had beautiful large white pines around our house. The houses were painted dark green on the second story and were white on the first floor with white trim. These colors seemed to blend the houses into the forest floor. Over the years, these trees sang me to sleep at night. I would open my window a crack, about two inches, and listen to them. The songs changed with how strong the wind blew or how bad storm was. I knew the squeak of a tree trunk bending a little too far in the wind and the crack of a limb breaking off. I heard the limbs breaking, the speed with which they would hit other branches on their way down, and then the limbs hit the ground with a whisper when it hit snow or a thud when big branches hit the ground. These are the sounds of a forest and living with a lot of pine trees in a yard.

In the fall, the pines would all lose their needles, which would need to be raked each year. We would rake the needles into rows and then make piles for pick up. We would load the needles by hand into Dad's trailer, which had high sides, and haul them out to the woods. While we raked, the pines dropped cones, too. I always loved to rake the pine needles as the smell was great. That wonderful smell would get into our clothes, hair, and nose. I learned quickly to wear gloves while handling the needles because bare hands would become covered with pine pitch, which is very hard to remove. We used gas on a rag to get the pitch off. I hated the smell. Today, we wouldn't have to use gas; we have "goo-gone."

The woods were non-ending around us. They were thick with different kinds of trees. Some areas had the same type of tree in clumps or they were mixed in with a lot of different types of trees. In the fall, the woods would make a beautiful painting with yellows, reds, oranges, and greens of different shades. There were oaks, maples, birches, ash, cedar, tamarack, balsam, fir, white pines, spruce and choke-cherries, which are the first ones to bloom in the spring and beautiful to see. The different types of trees grow in soils that they love. Some like dry, sandy soil, others like wet areas, some in regular field soil, and others in marshy lands.

Along with hundreds of pines, we had one ash tree in the yard. This tree was right on the line between the last neighbor's lot and ours. When the leaves fell in the fall, it was fun to rake them up, then run and jump into them. I loved doing that. The leaves would rattle and break, which released a woody smell, and the leaves became knotted in my hair. I spent a lot of time doing that in the fall. Dad would leave the pile until the very last before hauling it out. Usually I was in school when Dad picked the leaf piles up. It was a sad moment when I came home and the leaf piles gone. I played in the leaf piles until I was 14, which is when I discovered that I was too old and sophisticated for that game.

I started to learn the woods around us soon after we moved, and I learned to carry a long walking stick with me in the woods. Moving the stick back and forth in front of me can clear the trail ahead. Rattlesnakes will rattle or jump forward to bite, and better they bite the stick than you. Even garden snakes will move out of the way of the stick. I really never wanted to step on any snake. I hate snakes but learned how to live with them.

Wildflowers and trees became friends. I learned to identify trailing arbutus and found it in the spring, growing on the side of the hill coming down to the houses and Dam. It has a dark green waxy leaf and grows low to the ground, with branches running along the ground from the center of the plant. If you find some, smell them and then leave them alone. They are a protected plant, but that smell I will never forget.

Wintergreen grew on the hill by the dam site and most other areas I traveled in as well, even on the other side of the River. Wintergreen berries are close to the ground and are good to eat. Don't eat what you don't know. Some of the stuff can kill or make a person very ill.

Marsh marigolds grew in the swamps and low areas, and stream ditches running into the AuSable or even those along the road and swampy ponds. The marigolds bright yellow faces and large green leaves are beautiful. Other flowers I learned to identify were violets, colored purple, violet and yellow, which grew all over in the early spring. These along with white mayflowers really made the woods look great. Trilliums were all over as well and the spring was the time for mushrooms, which also grew all over both sides of the River. The flowers and mushrooms were dependent on the weather; they would dry up fast without rain. When the rains came at just the right time in the spring, the woods would fill with them.

Wild roses (pink) bloomed in the late summer and fall along the sandy trails running through our woods. They grew about three to four feet high, like a small bush, and would bloom on one branch. They have single petal flowers, but some branches would have many flowers on, while others would have only a few. Bees love the wild roses, and I would see them in the roses flying from flower to flower. White daisies and yellow brown-eyed Susan's grew along the roads to add to late spring early summer colors. Daisies grew on both sides of the Monument Road, from M-65 to Largo Springs.

I remember the day that I asked Mom to stop the car because I wanted to pick her a large bunch of daisies. She smiled and pulled over. I started to pick and soon I gave her a beautiful bunch of them. This was in June. With a gentle breeze blowing through them, the daisies looked like they were dancing in white dresses with yellow polka-dots. They still grow on that road, although they seem to be thinning out now. If you are lucky to be on that road at the right time of year, watch for them; they are beautiful.

Another plant that I started to identify was poison ivy. I have a story about poison ivy that's not really funny, but how it happened made it seem so, and because of who was involved. Mrs. Richeson was a very old lady, the mother of my Aunt Bertha's husband, Dr. Vern Richeson. They had all come up for a visit, and, as Mrs. Richeson was living with my aunt, she came too. Mrs. Richeson said she was going for a walk down our sidewalk behind the house and out to the road. Everyone was talking and time slipped away. Finally, someone said that Mrs. Richeson should have been back. Everyone went running for the door. I think everyone thought she had fallen in the River. When we got to the stairway down to the sidewalk in back, there she was holding the largest bouquet of poison ivy you would ever want to see, including yellow berries all over the stems.

As soon as we got our wits about us, my mother reached around on a shelf, grabbed a large paper bag and told Mrs. Richeson to throw the bouquet in.

"But why?", Mrs. Richeson asked. "They are so pretty. I want to put them in my Christmas wreath."

Mom soon told her why! Mrs. Richeson had to wash up with gasoline outside the house and then was taken to the basement where Mom washed her with Fels Naptha soap, followed by a washing with regular soap to finish. She was the cleanest woman in town!

I thought she should have known what poison ivy was at her age, but she obviously didn't. Mom called them in a week or two to see how she was. Aunt Bertha said Mrs. Richeson only got a small outbreak of poison ivy rash. She was lucky!

I never knew Mrs. Richeson's first name. When I was young and had to address an older person, it was always Mr. or Mrs. "whoever." That was the respectful way.

Another poison ivy story happened when a cousin, an older boy in his teens when I was young, came up for a few days. Rolland was around 18 or so. In fact, he was Aunt Bertha's adopted son. He also could not identify poison ivy. On this particular day, a warm, sunny one, he wanted to walk along the River. I showed him the path to follow and gave him a stick for snakes (of course), and off he went.

While on his walk, he went skinny-dipping in the River. When he came out of the water, he sat down on the river bank to dress before coming back to house. He never told us anything about what he had done or exactly where he had walked.

Two weeks later, he called and asked us to walk back along the path to see where he had been and to see if there was any poison ivy around. I went to investigate, and sure enough, I saw bent and broken poison ivy stems right on the bank where he had sat down. Poison ivy was thick in the area. Apparently, he had broken out all over his back side and around the inside of his legs. He was miserable, and it hurt to walk. It took a while to get rid of his rash, too.

Mom, dad, and I picked wild mushrooms, and I learned what to look for at an early age. The regular brown morel mushroom grew in our woods. The good morel is closed to the stem. But there's another mushroom that looks like the good one but opens at the bottom like an umbrella. At a certain stage, the bad ones can fool you, so I learned to be careful. I also found an area where the very large white morel grew. These are hard to find but are very good to eat. I also found the red, wrinkled mushroom that we called a beef-steak. We ate the good brown or white morel (both have closed bottoms). Some people also eat the red beef-steaks but many have gotten sick from them. They seem to sneak up on you. People can eat them with no trouble and then another time they get very sick. This happened to my mother. She had never let me touch the beef-steaks, but after her experience, she quit eating them completely.

I lived with a swamp behind the house, a very large one in front of the house directly across the river with yet a third one to the left across the dyke of the Dam on the other side of the river. We hunted all the time across the River. These woods were my playground. We looked for mushrooms in the spring, trapped, hunted in the winter, and walked through them in all seasons.

One day a neighbor came over after we smelled smoke on the wind. We were looking to see if we could locate what was burning. The neighbor told us that he had just heard of a bad forest fire by Mio, and that it was not yet under control. If the fire jumped the river, it would reach us. We waited. We continued to smell a lot of smoke, so we knew the fire was still active, but we did not see anything in the air. We were all standing in front of our house looking across the river and at the sky.

Suddenly, we saw the smoke, grey to black, rolling out from under the canopy of leaves across the river and on top of the trees at the river's edge. It was like a big wave coming out of the distance. As soon as the thick rolling wave of smoke reached the river, it completely disappeared. The wind was strong so the smoke went every which way and then was gone. It really got smoky, but we still didn't see fire. We were all ready to jump into our cars and leave if the fire jumped the river and started on our side of M-65. After seeing the smoke wave, we didn't see anything more. Finally, the calls came in that everything was out. We were safe, and we were all relieved. That was the only scare with fire that we had while living at the Dam house.

The woods change every day throughout the year. I would find the first plants and loved the fresh smell of woods in the spring. In the fall, woods have a different smell and sound, with the crunch of dead leaves underfoot. Ask a hunter about the importance of that sound! That sound is part of the hunt.

Take time for a ride down some of the back roads. Go slow. Some of the roads around the plains start to get sandy and can be hard to get through. But, go slow and roll your window down. Then stop anywhere and just listen. You'll hear and see a different world. Take the time to really see any woods, for what it is. They are all different.

Our woods and world are changing in many ways. Some of well-known trees are dying. , When I was growing up, I got to see them all at their best. I had the privilege of walking through them and learning about my friends the trees and flowers, sort of like a living book of knowledge. When I was moving to my new home on the AuSable River, I did not know it was to be a wonderful education.

EAGLES

When we first arrived at the dam, eagles were rare. When a nest of eagles was found, it was an exciting event. Dad, Mom, and I went up under the nest, which was on an island. We never touched anything. It was very quiet and nothing moved. The birds were very quiet or away from the nest. Under the nest and all around the tree trunk were the bones of all kinds of fish and small animals. It was also stinky. These birds are wonderful to watch in flight. They love to find an out-of-the-way place to build their nests. They fly around and bring food to nest. Eagles are a protected species, and their numbers have increased a lot. In the summer, they sit on top of light poles, looking for lunch or looking along the roads for car kills.

CHAPTER 10: MAKING DO

During the WWII, gas and sugar were rationed to help the war effort. Because of the long distances we had to get food, Mom shopped once a month and tried to get everything she might need for the month. She would use part of the fruit-room to store canned goods and bulk foods like rice, flour, and whatever sugar we could get.

There was an another one-track road that led up behind a store that sold groceries, souvenirs, and gas, and had small cabins for hunters and fishing people. This was on M-65 but instead of going up the big hill on 65, we could use this little one-track to cut some miles off when getting things, we needed. This would mostly happen toward the end of the month when we would run out of basic things like milk, butter, and eggs. In the winter these roads were not plowed, so we had to use the long way to Hale or do without.

This grocery store was known as the AuSable River store and was run by Frances and Helen Morton during my time on the River. Frances and Helen would bring things from Arizona for their jewelry line to sell in the store during the summer months. I used to look into their display case and dream. I wished I could buy every one of those pieces. My Uncle Dan, Dad's brother, came up once, and I went to the store with him. While he was looking for something in the store, he noticed me standing at the jewelry case. He bought me a bracelet, which I loved and kept for years, and I still love turquoise jewelry.

Every time we went to Hale, we passed through a small summer cabin area, as well as the Rollways Camp site before going through the village of "Evergreen Glades." For a long time, that village has had that small grocery store with ice cream and a bear in a cage. That store helped supply a lot of things and food to replace what people used or forgot to bring while up north. Otherwise, they would need to drive all the way to Hale.

At first, the bear was only in a cage. Then, the owners had to put a fence around an enclosed area, and after that a double fence. There was a story about the bear getting out and roaming around the village, until the DNR caught it. That was when the second fence was ordered.

We used to get ice cream cones there from time to time on our way home from Hale. Mom needed many things that this little store did not carry, so we usually shopped in

Hale, at the Pearsall store. Mom and Dad always enjoyed talking to the Pearsall's The Pearsall store had groceries on one side and hardware on the other.

Another place visited by mom was the Hale grain mill. The mill ground the chicken feed, had extra cotton bags to buy for making quilts or clothing and get fresh butter and fresh milk. These places are gone now.

At the back of the house, and across the road from our house, was our garden along with some fruit trees: four apple and one pear tree. The pear tree needed another one to help it pollinate, so it never produced many pears. What it did produce were good eating.   Our tree was a Bartlett Pear. Pears would be picked on the green side and left on a blanket or the floor to ripen. Once ripened, we canned them for a great treat in the winter. Today, I have three pear trees in my lawn because I love to eat them.

The apple trees were not taken care of, but we ate whatever we got year after year. The far tree had good apples and produced enough for the three of us. Mom made applesauce from it, but she never tried to store the other ones. I think now that they would have been good for pie apples later in the year.

The deer would come at night and clean up the ground of the fallen apples and pears. I remember watching them while lying on my bed and looking out the window. The deer moved like shadows because of the street light, and the buck's horns would catch the light and flash. Especially if it was raining or if the moon was full, the deer would be visible, standing there and chewing.

MOM'S CAKES

From first to fourth grade, on my birthday, Mom would bake a huge birthday cake and bring it to school. She made it in four rectangular meat loaf pans. That was her secret to making large beautiful cakes. Then she would layer them, using a cooked frosting between layers and all over on the top and sides. Then she used a flat frosting spatula to make peaks in the frosting. Sometimes it would be a cherry cake with pink frosting, sometimes a yellow cake with yellow frosting, but, the one I like best of all, was her chocolate cake with vanilla frosting.

She would cover a flat wooden board to bring the cake to school. All the kids loved my birthday and looked forward to having a big piece of cake.

At our last class reunion, the girls and I were talking and they all said how much they enjoyed those cakes. I wish Mom was still with us, as she would have enjoyed hearing that story.

THE CHOCOLATE ESCAPADE

One boring and lonely day when I was eight or so, I found myself looking for something sweet. All my candy was gone and there wasn't a donut or cookie to be found. Mom would shop for groceries only once a month, and this was toward the end of a month. I looked for ice cream in the freezer in the refrigerator. Nothing. What I really wanted was chocolate, and when I shut the refrigerator door, I spied Dad's bread box. He used it to store his cigarettes, cigars, gum cartons, and CHOCOLATE – Hershey's large candy bars with almonds! I had found something sweet to eat!

I thought, *Dad will never miss one piece from his box.* Still, the box was Dad's box and I knew it was wrong of me to take what was his. But, the drive for chocolate was too great to resist. Dad was sleeping upstairs at the time, so I very carefully opened the door and peaked in. There were two full bars of chocolate, and one had been opened and part of the bar was missing. Dad had already eaten sections of it. I took one of the sections out and decided, he'll never miss it. I ate my little piece very slowly, enjoying every bite!

The next day, Dad approached me and asked, "Janice, were you in my bread box yesterday? I looked down and never said a word, but I felt awful.

RAISING CHICKENS

Mom tried to raise a garden, but after losing her garden to deer several times, even after using "something that would keep the deer out," she gave up. The deer even dug up potatoes and carrots and ate them. That was when she decided to raise chickens instead. But she needed a chicken coop.

Consumers Power said "no" to placing a building directly under the lines, but if we wanted to clean out an area behind the lines and build a coop, they would not have a problem. So, we did. Mom spent a lot of time out there, cutting and pulling bushes and small trees. Dad cut the bigger trees and we used them for firewood. He helped on clearing more when he could.

Mom and Dad made a large pile of brush, sticks, and twigs in the middle of the chicken yard and set fire to it after a snow. After this, Mom came down with the worst case of poison ivy I ever saw. It took weeks to clear. She had blisters that broke and got to a different spot, which then broke out, creating more rashes and sores. She had to go to the doctor for shots and a salve for the terrible itching. Mom was bed-ridden for a week or more. Dad and I wrapped her arms and legs with towels and in two hours they would be soaked from the blisters breaking and weeping into the towels. The doctor thought she had gotten such a bad case because they had burned poison ivy in the pile and she was breathing in the poison smoke. She had it on her face, arms, head, and legs. She was very lucky that the doctor had something that helped.

Despite the poison ivy, Mom went on with the idea of raising chickens after she got well. Dad built a small chicken coop, and we started with Rhode Island Reds. These chickens laid wonderful brown eggs, and the chickens worked the yard, which poison ivy was still trying to take over.

The first year, Mom raised Rhode Island Reds, which laid large brown eggs, but we found out that many people did not like brown eggs. It was something about the color. We ate a lot of egg dishes that year. During the chickens second year, in the fall, the chickens had to be removed to make way for a new batch. Mom took ten chickens at a time, butchered and cleaned them for our dinners. We had a very small freezer by then, so when the chickens were gone, she would do another ten chickens and so on. She also sold some to friends. She had learned how to do this at home on her family farm.

During the Rhode Island Red year, I made one chicken my pet. She was the smallest chick when we got them and never grew much. But she always had a tiny egg in the nest when she grew up. I would put her in my coat pocket and go for walks with her. I did this very carefully, and I would stroke her back from head to tail, which she seemed to love. After a while, she out grew my pocket and I couldn't carry her any more. But she still went with me, following me all over the yard, and, if

I sat down, she would hop up on my lap to be stroked. She would "coo" when I stroked her and sit down tight on my lap or the ground. I could tell that she loved being petted.

I named this chicken "Beckie" because she would very gently peck at my clothes or hand. She never did it hard, just softly enough to know she was there. When she walked with me, she clucked and clucked. When I would say something, she would cluck back. She was a lot of fun. Mom told me that she finally sold her because the coop was really getting cold, and she was too much of pet for us to eat her. She was also too small to sell for meat, but the lady who took her kept her as a pet as well.

Mom had two ways, and old way and a new way, to kill chickens and she taught me how. We controlled the environment. The old way was to have two large nails nailed close together, spaced to fit a chicken's head inside. Then Mom put the chicken's neck between the nails and chopped the head off with a hatchet. The hatchet was a short-handled axe with only one-side sharp; the other side was like a hammer. Mom could use the hatchet with one hand. The head would fall to the ground, and the body would flop around the yard until the chicken bled out. Mom's new way was better, but there were times when it was hard to do as you will see.

With the new way, we would hang the chicken by their legs in the basement, over the double-vats sink, and used a long, tapered knife. We pushed the knife down the chicken's throat. They died quickly. After our chicken was dead, it was dipped into a pail of hot water and the feathers pulled off. We used a wide board laid across the vat and rolled the feathers into a bucket on the floor. We used another board to cut them up before taking them upstairs to cook or freeze.

In our next flock, we raised White Rock chickens, and I had a pet rooster. It was huge, must have weighed 25 lbs. or more. My pet White Rock rooster was the last to go out of the coop, but Mother had a buyer for some chicken, and I had asked for a new bathing suit. I had seen the suit in either the Sears and Roebuck or Montgomery Ward catalog, and it was a very nice one. I sure wanted that suit.

"If you want that suit you will need to kill that chicken," Mom said, meaning my White Rock rooster.

Down to the basement I went with my rooster. Mom had the basement vat all set up and was waiting for me to do it, but I found it very hard to do. I was crying and talking to the rooster, telling him "I'm sorry!" I told him that he would be cold in the coming winter because the coop didn't have heat, and it was already close to Thanksgiving. So, my bathing suit won. We never raised chickens again, but knowing how to butcher chickens taught me how to handle chickens on our own farm later on. But, that's another story, maybe. And I never made pets out of farm animals again!

CHAPTER 11: RIDING THE SCHOOL BUS

Many of us had long rides on the school bus, so we often played cards to pass the time. Some would do their homework, even writing, which I couldn't because of motion sickness. I had to do my homework after supper.

I was good-natured and friendly to everyone on the bus. Even some of the younger ones on the bus still remember me. But around the ninth grade, the boys noticed me as well. Mom taught me to be nice to everyone, so I found it hard to fight back when the boys harassed me. Besides I was so scared of being kicked off the bus that I endured a lot. Some boys had been kicked off and suspended for three days for fighting on the bus. The boys, now men, will know who they are if they read this book. Thanks, I will say, for all the nights of trying to save my scarves by having to undo millions of knots, only to have you tie them again the next day. The boys would pull my hair from the back, twist my arms over the back of the seat, take my books, etc. I endured this for an hour and half bus ride each way, but mostly at night. Finally, I hit one of them and that was the end of taking my things and messing with me.

There are many stories about my bus rides. Perhaps spending three hours a day on the bus was the reason. I add them here because it was a different world back then, and the bus stories are often like mini-versions of childhood adventures.

First, there were no seat belts, so we went from seat to seat, even when the bus was moving. We had rough, bumpy, dusty dirt roads, and the roads could turn into "washboards" at certain times of the year, and into ice rinks at other times of the year.

One day on Cooke Dam Road, we were going around the "S" curve when it was ice covered. This road was also downhill. Our bus driver would go "like a bat out of hell." That day he made the first curve but not the second. We plowed off the road through tons of snow and ended up right in the middle of a grove of poplar trees. The snow was deep and we were wedged in tight. We sat on the bus until another bus came from school to rescue us then continued to pick up the other kids still waiting at the other bus stops and finally to school. We did not have phones on buses then. Our driver hollered down the road to our very next stop and told the kids to run home and call the school for a bus to come get us out. A work crew came with the bus and when we got home from school that afternoon, we learned that they had to cut trees to get our bus out. They must have used a truck with a winch on it to pull that bus backward.

I also remember a deer episode while on the school bus. When I was in the second grade, I and all the little kids rode up front. As the rules went, we basically sat in order of our grades: Kindergarten through second grade were in front, next was third through fifth, then sixth through eight, and nine through twelfth grades in the very back. Moving toward the back was called a "rite of passage." I had just been picked up at 7:30 in the morning, when suddenly the boys already on the bus were yelling, "Stop the bus!" They had seen a wounded buck in the ditch on the way to my house, but hadn't been sure he would still be there when the bus came back out. The boys knew it was not normal for deer to stay still unless death is near, and they didn't want the deer to suffer. Plus, most of those boys wanted the meat for their homes. Winters were very long and hard for some of the families.

The driver stopped and five or six of the high school boys got out. No one had a gun but they had knifes. Four or five of the boys jumped on the deer's back and held his head up, while another sliced its throat. They put the deer out of its misery. Then, they cleaned out the deer and turned it on its stomach to drain. The bus driver gave them a rag to wipe their hands as the boys boarded the bus again, leaving the deer in the ditch for the time being. The smell of deer and blood was strong, and we probably all smelled like deer when we got to school.

This episode has always stayed in my mind. Years later I ran into our old bus driver and he told me the following: When he got to school, he borrowed someone's car and drove to his home in Glennie and got his truck, his deer license, and his gun, and went back to where the deer was. He tagged the deer, put it into his truck, drove back to Glennie, and hung it in his barn. Then, he skinned the deer so it would cool fast. Went inside and washed up, drove back to Oscoda and returned the car. He got back just in time to get into the bus and drive us back to Glennie. Later, they all had a big venison party, including the high school boys and their families, and divided the deer meat among the families.

All animals should be put out of their misery when possible. Once there's a bad shot or if an animal is found trying to run but is wounded, a hunter will not leave it. In such situations, animals are shot to end life in a humane way. Hunters do have a heart.

Another bus story has to do with a time I played sick. I was bored at school and wanted a day off. A forest fire stared in the south part of River Road while school was in session. School released early to get our bus through because the fire was moving quickly toward an area of River Road. Our bus was re-routed through a mile-square road, which was one-lane wide with sand and ditch on each side. This road was not built for two-way traffic. Our bus met a car going the other way and moved over. The sand started to shift from under it, like a landslide, and the bus slowly tipped over and ended up in the ditch, on its side. Another bus had to come to pick up and deliver the children home. Everyone was fine, no cuts. But I was mad. I had missed everything. I never played hooky again!

Another bus story had to do with my Mom. I was in seventh grade, and I did not really see this happen as the bus had just dropped me off at home. I was walking down Loud Dam Road when this happened. I heard all about it the next morning on the bus to school. On the sharpest curve on Loud Dam Road, the bus met my mother and ran her off the road. They had been in the same snow track, and Mom didn't want to hit a bus so she took to the snow on the right. The road was very sandy underneath the snow. The bus continued around the curve going out, while Mom was stuck in the snow and sand. She couldn't move the car, and there wasn't any help close by as all the summer people were long gone. The boys on the bus saved her. They saw what happened and told the bus driver to stop.

"We can't leave her," they said. "We'll push her out."

That's exactly what they did. It would have been a long way for Mom to walk, especially after working all day. She was always thankful for the help she got that night.

CHAPTER 12: SNAKES:

We had a number of different kinds of snakes in our area: garter snakes, green snakes, spotted adders, rattlesnakes, including the Eastern Mississauga Rattlesnake. Another one, according to Dad, was the "Timber Rattlesnake." The Timber snakes were longer, smaller around and rounder than the Massauga. Massauga Rattlesnakes were short, fat, had larger rattles compared to the Timber and had large, flat-looking heads with beady eyes. I have seen both, and only saw the Mississauga Rattlesnake once.

It was while I was riding my bike along the walking path in front of the houses. I noticed a movement in front of my front tire, saw the rattle snake, and only had time to pull my legs up. Over the snake I went. About ten feet farther, I stopped to see if I had hurt him. He just turned and went back down the hill toward the River. If I hurt him, I never knew about it.

I saw snakes in all varieties and forms, from three inches, nine inches, up to a foot or longer, in the yard and under the clothes lines, as well as in the woods. I mention the clothes lines because those are almost a thing of the past these days. For those who might not know what they are for: these lines are where we dried our clothes. The wind blowing through the clothes would not only dry them but also take out wrinkles without having to iron everything.

Mom would send me out with a basket full of clothes. This was before dryers were invented, and we used clothes pins to clip the clothes onto the rope or wire lines. Mom would be washing the clothes while I was hanging them up.

Before I started hanging them, I would walk the whole area first with a stick. I tapped and swept with my stick across the grass around the lines to scare the snakes into the tall uncut grassy areas. This tall grass area was where the third house garden plot was, but the neighbor never had a garden. Mostly, the snakes were small ones, but now and then, there was a large one or two. I sure did not want to have one bite me. Boy do I ever hate snakes! Later I found out why he did not garden. He was fighting a form of cancer. He also raised mink which was a lot of work to do. Any loud noise the mink would eat their young. When he got worse, he had to give up his mink farm.

The adult Michigan water snakes were about 5 feet long and small around. When in the water, they moved fast. The snakes would curl up on the log retainer walls (used to prevent a washout from the hill by the water coming from the dam). One day, I was walking on the log retainer wall fishing. Suddenly, I became aware I was not alone. There were snakes everywhere. I backed out slowly and never went there again!

Another snake story is about the snake that liked to live under my bed. This happened from second grade through high school. I called him "Fred." Fred would creep out in the night from the attic or from a hole in the corner where the wood wasn't quite together. I just knew he was waiting to bite me when my legs went over the bed. I was afraid to get out of bed to go to the bathroom. Mom finally gave me a flashlight to look before getting out, but even so, I saw "Fred" in my dreams, chasing me and getting closer and closer, and bigger and bigger. He had grown really big by the time I finally woke up. "Leave me alone," I told him. "Go back to your hole wherever it is!" That was my last nightmare, but snake movies will still give me a re-visit from Fred. I don't watch any snake films at all, real or not. Fred was not a real snake just a repeating nightmare!

Another snake story is about a Consumer's Power family picnic. Consumer's Power put on a picnic so that all the operators on the dams and their families could meet. At the picnics, there were games for kids, and grown-ups could see each other, put faces with voices, or meet those on different shifts who were doing the same job. But even during the picnics, someone was still at each dam working and couldn't come. I think they would rotate so that all the men eventually got to go. Swing shifts and life styles also made it so that the women couldn't be very socially connected, so the picnics weren't so much fun for them.

I remember one picnic that was held at the Pine River Campground rearing ponds. It was east of Glennie on F-30 (west of Mikado, turn on the sandy road to the south until coming to the Pine River and the campground site.) I'm not sure if the campground is still in use today.

Before we got to the picnic, one of the Consumer's men had killed a three-foot rattlesnake. It had an extra-long set of rattles. The dead snake was draped over the lower branch of a tree limb, so I got a good look at his head. I never saw one that big again. He must have had a good food supply to have gotten that big. Needless to say, the kids were kept away from the area by the water in case there was another one.

I have another snake story, and I do hope that Fred does not come back tonight to chase me again. Our road, from the bottom of the hill to the turn into our house, was full of rattlesnakes coming out of the swamp heading for the tall hill on the other side of the road. They were spread about two or three feet apart all going the same way, little ones and some really big ones. Those snakes looked like they were migrating, like the birds do, I thought!

It was spring and I had a two-wheel bike as usual. I wondered if riding over a snake would kill it. So, I tried! I put on my brakes right on top of a smaller one and slid across his body. He kind of rolled upwards into a coil, came back down, and crawled off the road. No, it did not kill the snake! I'm glad I hadn't fallen off the bike right then because there were enough snakes on the road that I would have been easily bitten. From then on, I used a shovel if snakes were in the yard...meaning I would kill them with the shovel.

Still, I wanted to see if I was right about riding over a snake. In the fall, I watched for a return of the rattlesnakes. Sure enough, there they came, slithering back into the swamp again. They all came (and went) into the swamp in one day. I thought it out and decided that temperature made this happen. In the winter it was warmer in the swamp. Some of the places never froze so the snakes went to the swamp to keep warmer. In the summer, they ranged all over in the woods, the River, and when it got colder in the fall, they would go for the swamp once again. In my head, rattle snakes migrate and I called this "the rattlesnake migration"!

Another snake encounter happened just after graduating from high school. I was home and decided to go swimming in the afternoon when the wheels on the dam were shut off. They had changed the times and the dam was running; the water was swift. I had always been able to swim upstream with the current, but then I had been swimming every day. Now I had lost that ability. I was swimming as hard as I could for the side so I could walk out before the mucky area along the River. I noticed a movement in the water about 30 feet ahead of me. It was one of the Michigan water snakes coming, with about six to eight inches of his head out of the water. He was looking for something to eat; his head turning right and left. I knew he was going to hit me and I didn't want to get bitten in the face. The only thing I could think of was to make a large wave with both arms to try to fend him off. It worked, but I felt his tail slide down one leg when the current pushed him by me. These snakes grow 4 – 6 feet long. I had seen water snakes slide into long retainment poles just below the dam on the right side many times. It still gives me the shakes, even as I write this story. When an area is no longer used, nature will reclaim it. In this case, snakes were taking over my old swimming hole. I never went back swimming there again.

CHAPTER 13: FRIENDS AND FUN RECESS

The swings and monkey bars were popular at recess, which, looking back we only had a few of them. The teachers wanted to keep the fourth through sixth grade kids off the swings and monkey bars to let the younger kids use them. So, the teachers formed girls' and boys' softball teams, boys against boys, girls against girls. Teams played across grades, or if there was a second team in a class, the teams would play each other.

When I was in sixth grade, we had the same system of teams, except that Delores Ellis and I were finally made captains of our teams permanently. All the girls could play because two teams were now formed. We all knew who had more experience and were the better players. Before, if Delores won the bat, she would pick me, and if I won the bat, I would pick her. When we played on the same team, the other teams could never win. By being captains, we could no longer play on the same team; it made the teams more equal. In seventh grade, we didn't have softball anymore. I always wished we could have continued, as I loved that game. We had a lot of fun running around the bases.

In the ninth through twelfth grades, we played basketball, half-court. Guards were not allowed across the court and the forwards were the same. We all wanted to play full-court like the girls do now. We did get to play different schools and that was fun. I don't have any great things that happened while playing, just that we did it and how. Some schools didn't offer any sports for girls! We were lucky.

MUSIC – PIANO – BAND

In the second grade, I started to take piano lessons with Joan Heine, my next-door neighbor. I learned my notes, the piano keyboard, and some simple songs. She taught me a few things but when she got busy with school, I switched to a teacher in East Tawas, Mrs. Hertzler. She gave lessons to a lot of children. Mr. Hertzler was a well-known lawyer in East Tawas.

By the third grade, I had improved enough to play from a small book of one- or two-page simple songs. By the fourth grade, I was losing interest in piano. I quit just before the start of fifth grade. Instead, I was going to play a tonette, which was how we joined band in school.

Doing both piano and band would have been too much to do.

Having had piano lessons really gave me an advantage for the tonette. Everything I had learned for piano transferred easily to the tonette; the notes and the beat were the same. I took to playing the tonette and carried it wherever I could. As soon as I learned what hole I needed to cover for which note, I was off and running. I was able to play very well.

In the sixth grade we were introduced to the instrument we wanted to play in the band. I chose the clarinet. I used a school clarinet with my own mouthpiece until the seventh grade when Mom and Dad bought me my wood clarinet. I used that clarinet through high school. Mom got tired of dusting the piano after I left to go to work in Saginaw and she sold it. I had learned to play The Blue Danube, which Mom loved. I played it when she returned from the hospital downstate, and I played it for her every now and then afterwards.

As a band member we used to play in the Oscoda band shell every Saturday night. To do this was time consuming. We had to practice all week at home on our parts, and we practiced together as a band on Tuesdays. Then Saturday night we took our places in the band shell and played the songs that had been picked for the week.

The band shell was located in the park close to the Oscoda township offices, which is now on the corner of River Road in downtown Oscoda. It was located on the south side of the first block from the light.

In order for the Saturday concerts to happen, an Oscoda Area Schools bus came to each of our houses to pick us up. The bus came down River Road to Loud Dam first, and then went up M-65 to Glennie turning east toward Mikado. We turned south on the road just before F-41, called Cruzen Road and picked up a lot of kids along the way and came out to F-41, picking up more kids all the way to Oscoda. The route was reversed going home, so I was always the first on and the last one off. I sure got tired out on some of those trips, depending on what else I did that day. This went on every week all summer long for practice on Tuesday and concerts on Saturday.

PHONE CALLS AND FEMALE TROUBLES

When I was in the sixth grade, I would get sick every month with "female problems," which I didn't want to have and didn't want to talk about. Sometimes I would get really get sick with terrible cramps.

One time I wanted to call Mom to come and get me. School was in Oscoda, 25 miles away and a long ride through bumpy, dusty gravel roads. To call her, I had to call Foote Dam, then ask for Loud Dam. I called, hoping that Dad was working, but I couldn't always remember what shift he was on. If he was working, I could tell him I was sick and why; dad was easy to talk to. I didn't want to tell that to all of the dam operators.

On this particular day, my luck wasn't good; Dad wasn't working. So, the operator called our house. At that time, our house phones were identified by the number of rings: first house; one ring, second house, two rings; third house, three rings, etc. When a phone started to ring, everyone along the line was alerted and waited to see if the call was for them. Anyone in six dams and three houses could be on the line.

I finally heard Mom say "hello," and told her I was sick. She never asked what the problem was; she only said "I'll come and get you. Just go lay down somewhere." She knew I was having trouble that I didn't want to mention and didn't question me. After that first time, we developed a code word for such situations. I really never had to call after that because if I wasn't feeling well, I stayed home. I loved school so sometimes I went anyway.

DAD'S MODEL-T

Dad got a Model-T fixer-upper. It had no doors, no top, half a front window, and only two seats. It was running but really needed an overhaul. Dad worked on it. He took the front window off completely, painted it John Deere green with paint given to him by a cottage owner. He got a bus seat and put it in for a back seat, so we had four seats and could all go for rides in it. We rode around with it every now and then. I liked riding in it because it was open-aired, but we had to watch for branches hitting us in the face. Dad always drove it slowly, giving it gas only when going up a hill.

Everyone loved the car and asked questions about it: Where had he found it? Where had he found the parts? Would he sell it? At some point, he did sell it. I remember coming home one day and the car was gone. Dad simply told me, "I sold it." Maybe he got enough money to part with his play toy. I remember one day while I was riding with him in the car, one of his friends on the road saw us.

"Don," he said, "you must have done really well since I last saw you if you have to drive that thing now!"

They both laughed and laughed. They looked so funny laughing that they got me laughing, too.

We had to put our thumb on the inside of our hand and turn the crank. They used to break a lot of thumbs when the machine would kick back. Wrists and hands were broken. Dad told me this when he taught me how to start it. We sure had a lot of laughs riding around in this car. It was a conversation piece and opened a lot of questions from people vacationing or fishing.

SLEDDING

In winter, I liked to slide down the dike. I sure had fun. One day, Mom and I both got on the sled and went down. I was on top of Mom and when the sled broke, I kept going downhill, straight into a soft snow drift, face and head first. Everything was quiet for a few minutes.

Mom told me that all she could see was a small circle of brown, which was my snow pants! Suddenly the snow went all over and I stood up, wiping snow from my face and laughing. We were both covered in snow. The next time we went sledding we took a toboggan. It could hold us both!! Dad told us what went wrong with the sled: "Both of you on that sled is too much weight. You are lucky you are ok!"

ICE SKATING

The water behind the dam and by the steep hill where people could get boats in and out was a great place to ice skate. Many times, in that area, the water froze over smooth, which made it great for skating. Sometime we would build bonfires on top of the ice to warm up. There was usually a wind blowing, which would cool the skater right down. Sometimes we just toughed it out and went home frozen. Sometimes a friend would come to skate with me for a few hours or Mom would go skating too. I went skating by myself many times.

When the dam released water from the backwaters, the water levels shifted, sometimes causing cracks in the ice. We would hear a loud cracking and see a crack running toward us at high speed. The crack would be about an inch or so wide. This scared me at first, but Dad said that it was ok and only an expansion crack. He also said the ice was strong and thick enough to hold us up. One day, a crack went between my legs, and there I was standing with a leg on each side of a crack. I wasn't so sure Dad was right! I turned and saw the crack just continue on and on, until it was out of sight. The cracking sound is what made me worry; it's loud.

One of the fun things we did was to take a blanket, each of us would hold a side, and make a sort of sail. I even found a way to do it alone. The wind would push, and I could go along the shore farther and faster when I had the sail. I would then wrap the blanket around me to skate back against the wind. The blanket gave extra warmth, but it wasn't as much fun. In fact, skating against the wind was hard work. That's usually when I quit skating and went home. By the time I got home I was beat! It must be a mile walking back to the houses.

I had a private spot through the woods behind the third house. It was a lot warmer in there for skating, and there were logs to jump and trees to skate around or swing on. The boys in the first house used to clean out that area so they could skate there. The boys grew up and left home, and I wasn't about to wade into knee-deep water and muck in the spring and fall to pick up limbs from the trees that had dropped them in the water, and trees fell in, too. So as things fell into that area, it became harder and harder to skate there. The ice was always smooth because the wind never got in to rough up the surface as the water froze.

SWIMMING

I had a nice swimming place behind the houses at Five Channels. It was nice because there was sand on the bottom. The older kids at Five Channels, kept the weeds out, and the water level went down gradually, so young children could learn how to swim there. This is where Mom taught me to swim. Later, when I really knew how to swim, I was allowed to swim in front of our house. I swam at the house until the snake and I met eye to eye.

I liked to swim when the wheels were off on the dam, as I could take my time and swim in circles, or up and down as slowly as I wanted. When the wheels were on, I had to swim arm over arm, like walking on a treadmill today. This was just to stay in place, and it was hard to gain on the River current. By the twelfth grade, I got good enough and strong enough that I could swim upstream a little, fighting the current. The water in front of our house was sixteen feet deep or more. The AuSable is a big, deep river in some places.

We tied a boat up in front of the house. We had a motor for the boat but usually I rowed it wherever I wanted to go. I knew some good fishing spots that were close by and it was fun to row around the River.

ROLLER SKATING

From about the time I was 12 to 14 years old, Saturday nights were spent roller skating in Hale and Tawas. I skated in both places off and on, and I loved it. During this time, the owners would have all the couples go out first, then they would tell the extra guys to choose a girl. If they couldn't get one to skate with, the boys would line up with the left-over girls. Periodically a light would flash, and when it did, one person would go toward a couple skating and one of the partners would have to trade. The trade would always be with the same gender waiting, and the other boy or girl would have to go wait in line until he or she could get out there again. This often went on for a while before someone could go back skating with their original partner.

I remember a very good skater at the Hale rink. He really knew his stuff! One night, he skated with me, out of the blue. It sure was fun to get guided around with the rink with him almost like dancing. That was the first and last time for me. He didn't come after that as he moved or he may have gone to war.

HORSES

Just past Evergreen Glades on the large curve is a road going west. On this road was a riding stable where I would go from time to time. This was when I was 14 to 15 years old. I would ride a pony that was the love of my life. That pony would do whatever I asked. Mom would drive me to the stable and read while I rode for an hour.

I loved those times. The pony ran, jumped, and followed the trail with her reins loose, without me even guiding her. Plus, I talked things out with her. Her ears would be up and go backward and forward. I knew she was listening. Sometimes when we came to a fork in the trail, she would stop and look back at me for directions. She was some horse! I will never forget those days with her.

One day, I went to ride, and the owner told me I was too big to ride her anymore. He was going out of business and only had "my" pony and the horse he rode. He said he would let me ride his horse, and put me on his big stallion. The stallion had huge feet, evil eyes and a very large head. I had to watch him every minute, and he didn't want to go with me on right from the first. I fought him all the way down the lane. He seemed to have made up his mind to take me where I wanted to go, but when I got to a fork, I made a big mistake.

I let him have the choice of which fork to take, like I had often done with the pony, so I loosened up his reins. He grabbed the bit in his teeth and turned so fast that he almost threw me off the saddle. I managed to get myself back in the seat and hung on, as he headed straight for the barn door, a double one, with the bottom open and the top closed. This was a very large horse and he was planning to scrape me off his back going through the bottom door.

As we rounded the turn going into the barn yard, and as I was getting my feet out of the stirrups so that I could jump off, the owner shut the bottom door. He had heard us coming and knew I was on a runaway horse. The horse put the brakes on, and because my feet were out of the stirrups, I almost went over the horse's head. It was a close call. The horse skidded up to the barn door and had to turn his head so he wouldn't hit it.

Needless to say, I got off right away and the owner took the horse. The stable was put up for sale shortly after so that was my last ride. By then, I was involved in school activities. Times were better; I was learning to drive, my time was spent in band, basketball, and with a boyfriend – the three B's.

RADIO AND TV

We couldn't get radio reception at the Dam. Off and on, we could pick up radio stations in the car, but whenever we went under the electric lines, we lost reception for a while. But the main electric line was right beside the house, so we got a short-wave radio. After we got the short-wave, we could hear the boats on Lake Huron talking to each other. We also heard WWII speeches and some of Hitler's speeches, too. We also had some music channels, and heard of the bombing of England by the Germans.

Finally, television came in and our first one was a black-and-white. I was in the 8th grade before Mom and Dad saved enough money to buy one. It was hard to keep the picture on the screen. The picture would roll up and down, sometimes fast, sometimes slow. So periodically we would have to go over to the T.V. to adjust it so the picture would stay put. Most of the time, by the time we got back to our seat, the picture would be back to rolling again. Back and forth, we would go, until we gave up and went to bed. If we got lucky and the picture stayed on a slow roll, we just pieced the picture together in our minds.

Sometimes it rolled really fast or went black and had only voice. Or, it was in various shades of snow flickering on the screen with or without the voice. Weather conditions caused a lot of the bad reception. Color television didn't come in until after I was married.

As bad at T.V. reception was, when it did come in right, it was wonderful. Now we had movies in the house. We watched Bob Hope, Dean Martin, Jerry Lewis, Sid Caesar, Jackie Gleason, Jack Benny, and Loretta Young, dressed in beautiful dresses, as she floated through the door to introduce her show. There were also full-length western movies cut down to fit the television time slot.

We also had a Victrola with a crank. We would wind it up to play a record on the turntable. After cranking, we would pick up the arm with the needle on it and place it carefully on the record. These records did not have the clear sound that we do today; they were scratched and sometimes skipped.

After I went to work, I bought a record player on credit and made payments. I could play 78 rpm records, 33-1/3, or single 45s. This was in 1956. I was living in Saginaw at the time and left the record player home with Mom and

Dad so they could play while I worked to pay it off. They really loved that record player. Dad built an outside speaker so we could play music outside while working or for Christmas. Elvis was just getting his start at the time. Tennessee Ernie Ford and Nat King Cole were always playing.

MOVIES

I was in grade school when Mom had to pull me out of the East Tawas movie house on Main Street during playing of the movie, "Lassie Come Home". It had just come out and had been sent to a lot of theaters across the country. All the kids were talking about going to the Oscoda Theater to see it. We were going to Tawas so we saw the movie there. The Tawas Theater was packed wall to wall the night we went. When Lassie died, I was overwhelmed and I started crying and sobbing uncontrollably. It took Mom quite a while after we left to convince me that it was only a story, that it was not real and that Lassie was still alive in real life. I finally settled down, but I never went back to see Lassie again.

Westerns were always the love of my life because of their beautiful settings and the horses. Roy Rogers, Dale

Evans, and Trigger were my all-time favorites. Trigger was a one of a kind horse, and did many tricks for Roy. Roy even said later in one of his interviews that he "never had another horse like Trigger."

Later on, it was John Wayne for westerns, and Clark Gable was the man I was going to marry, tall, dark, and handsome. That was not to be; I married a better one, a sandy blonde-haired man with a sense of humor.

POLIO'S EFFECTS

While I was in the fifth grade, we had a life-changing event that affected the whole class. We lost a classmate, Carol Ann Robinson, that October. Carol was a real close friend of mine, and we sat together in the row by the window in school. I had a birthday party that October at a cabin resort on the beach in Oscoda, and we invited all the girls in my class. We had the party in Oscoda because it was too far to drive to the Dam for some of the girls.

At the party, we had tons of fun, playing games outside, hitting beach balls and talking. Mom had some inside games for us, too, with prizes and her wonderful birthday cakes. The girls brought presents and I opened them. Soon after, the girls were picked up, one by one, by their mothers. The party was over, Mom and I, mostly Mom, cleaned the cabin. This was on a Saturday.

The following Monday, Carol was late getting to school, and when she came in, she looked sick. She said she had an awful headache and didn't feel well at all. Saturday, at my party, she had been feeling great and we had had fun playing and laughing together. On Monday when Carol got to school, our teacher saw her coming and walked to the door. I also saw Carol and walked over to meet her, and we walked to our seats. A half hour later, Carol said that she was feeling worse and wanted to go home. I told the teacher and Carol left the class. That was the last time we saw her.

On Wednesday, the teacher and principal came to our room and told us that Carol had died. This was a shock! As an only child, I thought if Carol had died, it could easily happen to Mom or Dad. During that time, we were going through war-time drills too, I was scared because we had drills and were taught to sit under our desks if a bomb went off. We also were taught that if we heard a three-bell warning, we were to line up, go to the hall, and sit with our backs to the wall. This was in case of tornados. There was a two-ring bell also for bad weather, I think. We were all stressed from the drills, and how we had to deal with the death of a classmate. It was hard.

I knew that I and my classmates were in grief, but I didn't understand what that was. Carol's brother had had the same illness and was in the hospital with it when Carol lost her life. Her brother came back with his legs severely deformed. He was walking with crutches the last time I saw him.

Later, teachers told me that our class was watched very carefully for signs of illness because we had all been together at my party. They expected an outbreak of polio meningitis and they didn't know where it was coming from. It wasn't until the seventh grade that we got vaccinated for polio. We got the vaccine in a sugar cube. In the seventh grade, we had another classmate come down with polio, but she was able to recover enough to get around on her own. A lot of children and adults, too were put inside what they called the Iron Lung, for the people to breath in. It forced the air into the lungs. One teacher's wife had one. His name was Mr. VanCamp.

The affected person lived in this apparatus day and night. Some could get out briefly but when their oxygen level dropped, they had to go back in.

Little House

Dad carving a pumpkin with me

Mom, fish and Dutchie

Me Picking Daisies.

Me holding Peggy, Uncle Dan Weinberg, Dad, Uncle Dan's son Rolland Weinberg

Dad, his car, and Peggy the dog

Bob took this picture of me from the boat in the middle of the AuSable River. We were picking up fishing lures.

Dad and the largest otter he ever trapped

Me, my mother, and my birthday cake

CHAPTER 14: FISHING, TRAPPING AND HUNTING

Our house was on a high bank so we had to walk to the bank to see the River. The River wasn't very visable from the house. Across the River, the land was lower. Wild life was everywhere: deer, bear, otter, beaver, muskrat, squirrels, bobcats, partridge, raccoons, skunks, porcupines, and snakes of many kinds.

As soon as we were settled in at the Dam, Dad gave me a rod and reel. I still have the pole. I had to fix one eye in it, and because I couldn't find a glass eye replacement, I had to use something else. I had to use a modern eye and Bob, my husband, welded it on for me. It still works. Even though it's not original now, it still catches fish, even in Canada.

Dad taught me how to tie a hook to the line, how to use swivels for the sinkers, and how to use a three-way set up, a hook on one corner with a lead and a sinker with a longer lead on it for the second part of the hook-up, and the line to my pole on top. For small fish, what we called pan fish such as small bass, perch, and blue gills, we used small hooks. For bigger fish, we used the boat for trolling and all kinds of lures. At first the lures were made from wood; later, they came in other materials. I was not allowed to fish by myself until I learned to swim. When I was finally able to fish by myself, I got my own tackle box.

When I caught something and kept it, the rule was "if you catch it or shoot it, you clean it." At the time, I remember thinking I'll never use all this knowledge; my husband will be doing these jobs. As it turned out, I've used this information all my life. My husband would have cleaned fish as he did deer over the years, but because fish are slippery, he never could handle them. He had had an accident at 11 months old that took his left-hand index finger off and made the two next stiff. Somethings, but not very many, are impossible for him. So, when we got married, I did all the cleaning of fish even on our Canadian fishing trips.

I have one of my early lures, sitting in my china cabinet. I call it "Sure Shot." It has a red head with glass eyes, yellow body (where the paint's still visible). It earned retirement. Sure Shot has caught many, many walleyes – on the AuSable, in Canada, and in the Upper

Peninsula of Michigan. I have always used it for trolling, never for casting. For casting, I used spoons mostly or a frog, catching pike up under those lily pads. The pike were just waiting for a frog or small fish.

To me, fishing has always been very relaxing and fun. The air is fresh and clean, but it can get mighty cold on the water on a summer day, so I learned to take a coat of some kind, along with some matches and paper to start a fire to keep warm in case of motor trouble.

On our lakes, boaters helped others but if no one else is around, being prepared could be handy. In Canada, it's a must-have. On the AuSable there are usually people around in the Loud Dam area and the backwaters there's not as many. Around Mio, there are probably a lot of people in the summer but when the kids start school, I would bet that the River traffic is next to nothing.

TRAPPING

When I first got interested in hunting, my father would take me with him early on to walk through the woods along the River in the spring and early fall. He was six feet tall, with long legs and size 12 shoes and could really step out. He carried a trapping basket on his back. In it, he carried everything to set or re-set a trap. At first, I found it hard to keep up with him. My short legs made it impossible to cross over the fallen trees like he did. I would have to sit down on the tree, turn around, put my legs on the trunk, turn to the other side, and hop down, before I could stand up and follow him. Most of the time, he was waiting, saying, "Are you coming?"

I did this with him about three times before I discovered some things about trapping. In addition to panting to keep up, it was wet, cold work and very hard to do. Besides, I never liked the way beaver and muskrats were trapped. Traps are opened up and set in an area where beavers are working. The signs we looked for cut limbs, fallen trees, or fresh limbs floating in the water. Another way to know was the way they built their houses up against the river or a large tree close to the river. Once we found such signs, we set the trap. Putting them by the bank, we rubbed the scent of a male beaver gland all over them, which would draw beaver into the trap. Dad got the scent from a previously trapped beaver. Then we drove sticks, like the size of canes, into the ground and wrapped wire around the canes and traps to hold them in place. When the trap went off, it would scare the beaver. It would dive into the river to safety. Instead the beaver would drown because the trap chain was short and wouldn't allow the beaver to come up again. This was cold hard work; I didn't like the way beavers were trapped, plus they really stink.

Dad would bring them home and stretch the hide on boards made especially for the hides. There were small, medium, and large size boards. The size used would depend on the size of the beaver. Dad would stretch and nail the hides to the boards. Then we would begin to scrape their hides. All the fat had to come out and the trick was not to go through the skin. After it dried, the hide was stiff. Dad would take the hides to a place where the hides were sold. When I was between thirteen and fifteen, I was trusted to do scraping.

I helped but I have never forgotten the strong smell. The fur of a beaver is very shiny and very soft and thick. Otter fur is even softer. They both were used for hats and coats at that time. They were shipped to all parts of the world but usually to parts that were cold. These furs have insulating quality and very warm to wear.

Dad also trapped otters because their pelts were worth a lot more money, but they were very hard to catch. Otters are playful and cunning and I liked watching them. They loved to swim in the River below the dam with the wheels running. In the spring it was fun to watch a mother otter and her young ones play in the current with each other. They are really a family unit. The little ones loved to roll in the water chasing their own or another's tail.

The young ones would also ride on their mother's back when playing, when danger was close or when they got tired. They loved to slide down the dike hill on the other side of the dam. When they slid down on their bellies, they all used the same slide path. They could run very fast even with their short legs when they thought they were in danger.

PARTRIDGE HUNTING

Dad knew that partridge would come out at a certain time of day and sit by the road, about 25 feet back in the fire lines. Dad told me his plan; I would shoot while he drove. He told me to look a certain distance back from the road where the partridge is. Away we went, Dad driving and I riding shot gun. Dad started driving slowly down the road; I was looking and shooting. Before we knew it, we had six partridge in our trunk. We went home and waited for Stan Wager, Dad's nephew.

Stan had a well-trained hunting dog and challenged Dad stating he could get more partridge with his dog. Dad said "He didn't need a dog to find the partridge. Dad had chosen the areas to hunt and now we were waiting from them to get back. When they came back the score was six to zero. Stan never said anything to Dad again about needing a hunting dog!

Mom got the worst part. She disappeared to the basement and when she came up, the birds were washed and ready to cook. She put them in the refrigerator overnight to cool and the next day we had a feast.

Partridge is a dark-meat bird, not white like chicken. They also have a wild taste to them, but I loved them.

What we did was not legal, so I don't do it anymore. I found this out when I was getting my deer license and read the small-game booklet. That didn't seem to bother Dad at the time, or maybe he didn't know. Who knows! Everything was food for hard times.

DEER HUNTING

At the age of fourteen, I started to hunt with Mom and Dad. I practiced shooting with them both, but mostly with Dad, until I could shoot well, load my own gun, and take care of it. He trained me in how to find my way out of the woods, how to use a compass, to use sounds to get directions, like listening for cars on M-65 or the dam horns, and to look where the sun was in the sky. In my area, I could hear cars on the M-65 or on Loud Dam Road and when the Dams blew their horns. He told me to listen for a barking dog across the River, and to follow a stream the way it flows because it was going to hit the River somewhere.

Dad taught me how to clean my gun and take care of it. I had to put it back in the gun cabinet after each use! It had to make sure it was dry first, wiping any moisture off with a rag and setting it out to air-dry.

When I was growing up, we could cross the River over the top of the dam. Loud Dam had a cement roof with three steps down to roof level from the dike area on each side. We would walk on the dike to the end and then on to a small trail that led to a Consumer's Power maintenance road. Today, they may use off-road vehicles to get into these areas. The other way to cross was to use a back road that we were told led to Five Channels Dam. It was a one-track road, but, because of a swamp area, this road was unsuitable for cars. This was a "corduroy" road, as they lay logs down side by side for a block or more across the middle of the swampy area. We always walked the middle, so it was sort of a path as well.

Where I hunted was off this road in the woods. Dad's and Mom's seats were on a path that joined my path. Dad marked the tree with a hatchet to find his way in before daylight. The part beyond his seat was the bad part of the road because they used horses to pull timber out of the woods. Nothing else could go in. The logs were rotten from being in the water all the time. It is amazing how the lumbermen worked around the woods in all kinds of weather. They were a strong bunch of men because of it.

After the swamp, the land goes up a small incline to higher ground and curves right. I used to turn left onto a well-worn trail. This was as far as I ever walked so I cannot write what was beyond this point, but I can tell where the path goes that we were on.

Along the trail, about 100 feet more or less, there was a large white pine along the side of the trail. In fact, we walked by the tree but never under the tree; we always circled the tree in a large circle. The tree had many scars on its side, as many bears, over many years, had marked this territory as their own. Dad showed the different marks on the tree. All male bear who rule an area do this, and all the females are their charges. Now and then a new mark appears on the tree, and this means that another bear has taken over, making this his kingdom.

The animal world is fascinating to watch, as each species has its own rules of life or death and of possession over an area. I never saw a bear while hunting in this area. Dad taught me never to go close to the big tree. Hunters trapped bears by putting meat over a branch, hanging it with a rope, and putting a trap under the meat on the ground. When the bear stood up to reach the meat, it would step into the trap which snapped closed. The bear couldn't get away and was stuck there until the hunter came back to shoot him.

After hearing this, I made up my mind early that if I saw a bear he would just walk by and I would watch. I always loved to watch the animals in the woods. They run and play like children or look for food to carry home. I hunted with a shotgun with slugs so the deer would have to be close for me to kill one. With bear, I would only have made him very mad. I had to go to Canada to see bears in the wild. They are an awesome animal. Mother bears are very protective of their cubs, and it's best to stay away.

I never got close enough to a deer to shoot one until after I got married. In part, this was because all the deer I saw at the dam were beyond my range. I only had a double-barrel shotgun with slugs so my range was short, although I did take the top off a small pine once! I saw a deer, tried a shot, but got buck fever with the shakes so bad that my shotgun was pointed in the air before I even pulled the trigger. The deer just walked away.

While I was training with Dad, I asked him where the best place was to shoot a deer. His answer was, "right between the eyes." His eyes twinkled when he was pulling my leg or kidding around, and that's what his eyes were doing with this answer. Well, I never got a chance to shoot a deer, but he taught me how to clean one, and I had to use that skill later in life.

My training was reinforced when I was 15 years old and one of our older hunters wanted to hunt the plains. I asked whether I could try hunting on the plains with them. Dad said, "Sure, I'll take you out". He told me to the ready to go in the morning and that we would hunt until 4:00 p.m.

I packed a lunch and we left for a spot Dad had hunted before. It was quite a drive. I remember that we went across Five Channels Dam toward Glennie and then turned left into the fire lanes again. How far we were or where we were at, I still don't know.

We parked the car along the road, and Dad led, all of us walking in single file. After a short way in, Dad stopped and told me, "Janice, you stay here." We will pick you up on the way out.

I found a log to sit on and stayed there for a while, but my legs were not comfortable. I looked around for another place to sit but didn't find anything else. While looking around, I realized that I could pick up the sticks and logs that lay on the forest floor, cut some branches and make myself a comfortable seat in no time. When I finished, I sat; I sat all day. I saw nothing, not a bird, not a squirrel, nothing!

As the afternoon drew on, it began getting dark in the woods and Dad had not come yet. As it got darker and came on 5:00 p.m., I still didn't see them. I wondered if they had gotten a deer and were slowed up by having to clean and drag it out. That's also when I realized that I did not know which way to go to get out. I should have marked the tree on the side away from the car first, and put a different mark on the back side so that I could tell where I had been when I first sat down. Tree marks show for a long time, even after dusk. Even breaking the lower branches half way off would have been good. Picking up things for the seat made me lose my directions as I had turned so many times for dead wood on the floor of the woods.

Another half hour went by; it was 5:30 p.m. and still no Dad. I was thinking that as I had paper and matches with me, maybe I should be building a fire for the night. One thing Dad had always said to me, "When you are lost stay put!" As I was thinking about my situation, I heard a different sound way far away. I stopped and heard my heart beat. No, I thought, it must be something else." I waited, listening intently.

There it was again. The sound was still way far away but it was a whistle. I wondered whether that was Dad or a stranger. I thought that Dad would show up any minute. Then, I heard the whistle again, but this time it was farther away. That's when I knew: it's Dad and he's lost. I blew my whistle as hard as I could. I heard the whistle again, now coming from behind me and closer. I answered. In a little while Dad walked up. I was happy to see him.

Dad just said, "Do you remember where we came in from?"

"No Dad, I thought you knew where you were going."

Dad, George the other hunter, and I walked over to a small road, which Dad said would run to the big one. It might be a long walk, but we would find the car, so that's what we did. At least we were together. As we walked, the night was coming fast. The small road ended a short way down at another road. We looked left – no car. Then we looked right, and only about a quarter to half mile away was our car.

Dad never said a word about this hunting trip to anyone, as far as I know, and he never took me hunting in the plains with him again. I think he was scared that he might have lost his daughter out there.

I learned never to trust anyone else to be my direction-finder in the woods. After this, I always stayed aware of where the car was. Every time I moved; I would make note where the car was located. Everything looks the same out there so unless a person knows where she's at, the best policy is to stay put. Dad was lucky that I had my whistle with me to lead them back to me and to the road. But I was lucky, too. It would have been a cold night to camp out.

The following story jumps ahead a few years. In September 1977, my father passed away. I inherited my father's rifle. That November, two months after his funeral, I was sitting on a runway near a small stream on the farm when I heard a deer coming. I could tell he stopped to drink but he was out of sight. I heard him jump over the stream, and he popped into view. It was a buck and the only shot I had was "right between the eyes." There he lay, my first deer! First, I laughed, thinking of Dad, and then I cried. The next year the very same thing happened in the very same spot -- another deer "right between the eyes".

I didn't have anyone to take over and clean this deer. Bob was home to clean my first one but this one I had to do it myself or the deer would spoil. I had to go home, hook up the tractor and trailer and drive back to the spot. It took me three hours to clean the deer. I kept getting sick to my stomach every time I made a move, from pushing in the knife to open the deer, to pulling the entrails out and smelling the strong smell scent of the male deer.

Every little while I would have to stop, vomit, then start again, repeating this until I finally cleaned him up as well as I could. I pushed him up on the trailer by myself. He was heavy! I drove the tractor and the trailer with the buck to the back of the house, ready to hang him up in the workshop with our chain fall. That was when Bob came home.

I was very thankful because Bob finished the project! I have not been hunting since! I can't eat venison anymore either. I think it's the iron in the meat; I cannot take anything with iron in it. Maybe it's because I really don't ever want to have to deal with cleaning a deer again. I had to laugh both times. Dad had been right, the deer had just dropped and stayed there when I shot them "right between the eyes".

CHAPTER 15: SUMMER JOB

By the age of 14, I wanted a job! I thought doing something would be better than sitting around home. So, I asked the owners of the Lumberman's Monument store if they needed help. They were surprised because no one would drive to the monument to work for the pay they could offer, and it was only a summer job with weekends in the fall. Summers were long for me, as we never went anywhere, and, because we shopped in Hale not Oscoda or Tawas, I never saw anyone I knew. I was hired.

What I didn't know was that they decided to put me in the log cabin by the Monument to work by myself. No one told me what I needed to do; I learned by doing. The cabin sold some jewelry, things with Lumberman's Monument written on, post cards, and other knick-knacks. Some days I sold a lot and would need more for the next day. Other days were slow and I only had one or two customers who wouldn't buy anything.

I also picked up and did general housekeeping in the cabin, and I had to wash the restrooms, which took time and was a terrible job! People sure can make a mess. When five o'clock came, I checked to make sure that no one was left in the restrooms and locked the door. I carried the fishing tackle money box back to the owners at the store every night. I had to go through the woods and across River Road. After I closed, there weren't any restrooms open on the cabin side, although people could walk or drive over to the main souvenir store to use the restrooms there – until that store closed. After that, it was the woods or nothing.

Both the cabin and the main store were run by Mr. and Mrs. Martin. In the summers, Mom would drop me off at the Monument before she went on to East Tawas. Mom was an excellent sewer, and she worked and taught lessons at the Singer Sewing Machine shop for a while. Later, she worked as a cook at Whispering Pines, which was closer. On her way back, Mom would pick me up, as we were always only a one-car family. Dad always walked to work, of course.

The job at the Monument made me some money to use for school clothes, shoes, etc. It also taught me to work for people and how to talk to people. I would tell customers stories about hunting and fishing, and how to find each dam. I had learned a lot from Dad.

In this part of my life, it sounds like Dad and I did a lot together, and we did at first. As I grew up, it seemed like he didn't know how to treat me. I remember one time that some deer hunters brought me a box of candy. I was taken aback in my shock. I had never had this kind of present before. I stood speechless for a moment, then heard Dad, "What do you say, Janice?" I quickly said thank you to the deer hunter and ran, crying to my bedroom. I was having trouble with my emotions around my time of the month, and Dad's reminder had made me into a small child again. I wanted to be grown up and be treated like one!

DISTANCE, DRIVING, COTTAGE/SUMMER PEOPLE

Distances were a big factor in my life. Hale was eleven miles away; Oscoda and Tawas were around 25 miles away. Our isolation limited what I could do, especially when Mom and Dad were busy. I couldn't wait to be able to drive.

When I was turning fourteen, Dad took me out in the plains to practice driving. Of course, now and then I had driven on some of the rides we had done, but now Dad was teaching what I needed to know for the driver's test: How to handle the car on sandy roads; how to pass on those roads; what to do on corners; to stop at stop signs; how to park in town, and always to be cautious. Backing up was another part. We practiced out there until I passed Dad's inspection and he declared that I was road-worthy.

I had to go to the Tawas City for my license and to take the road test. The Sheriff was there. He looked at me and said, "You look like you can drive. Can you?" Of course, I said "Yes." I drove out of town with my parents that day, with no road test. Boy, I was really proud that day. Dad was my only driving school instruction that I received!

Besides the distances, money was tight, so it was a real treat to drive to the movies once a week. Hale, a 22-mile round trip, showed the older movies, so the younger set liked to go to Oscoda or Tawas, a 50-mile round trip. Plus, there was a drive-in movie where we could eat popcorn in the car and all the cars were on an incline so everyone could see the screen. The drive-in had first run movies a lot.

Having cottage people who were friends with my parents was hazardous to me. I was always timid going up or down Loud Dam Road. If I went too fast, Dad's friends would tell him. Eventually, Dad started calling me "lead-foot." Looking back, I can see that there was a community raising me, but at that time, I didn't like this at all. I wished nobody told Dad on me, but I did slow down, some.

When I look back on life then, it's amazing to see how times have changed. I used to ride my bike up and back the whole road into the dam. I never worried about some stranger kidnapping me. In fact, I thought everyone was a new friend and could be trusted. In today's world, I do not think I could be as trusting.

When I first started to drive to and from Oscoda at night, I never had any worries about something evil happening. I always wondered what I would do if the car quit out on the road, with no phones and few people. Dad or Mom of both would pick me up after whatever I was going to a lot. We shared one car and so they would pick me up after the school activity.

I have never owned a car and I am now 80 years old. Dad owned our cars at home and when I needed it, I used it, until Mom or Dad had to go somewhere. Since then, I've been married and my husband Bob owns the car. (But I own the boat!)

Every time I left home, Dad would tell me, "be sure you are back before dark." I always sensed that the saying came from his family somewhere and he was passing it down.

THE CANOE RACES

Canoe races on the AuSable from Grayling to Oscoda have been going on for a long time. They are fun to watch and to follow the canoes from dam to dam to see how they are doing. At home I would take a chair out to the river bank and watch as the canoes went past. At first, we waited at the back waters until the canoes pulled out and were carrying their canoes down to put in below the dams. We would watch the first ten or so canoes do this, and then go watch them from our yard. Eventually the races became more and more popular and the River bank became crowded, so we just watched from our house. At every dam, the canoeists have to carry their canoes around each dam and then put in again. A canoeist gets very tired before reaching Oscoda. Speed, skill, and stamina is what wins. Over the years, a lot of our school alumni were in the race, so it was fun to watch.

HIGH SCHOOL & TEACHERS

We had great teachers at Oscoda High School. It's hard for me to pick just one to write about. One special one was Mrs. Virginia Hans because she went so far out of her way for us girls. In the sixth grade, for one class we split into two sections: boys went to gym and girls stayed with Mrs. Hans to learn to sew, by hand. She cut the patterns out for us and we made the marionettes. Each was different. There were fairies, kings, etc. Mine was a witch, and I thought she turned out great.

My witch was in a black dress and black shoes, which I cut out and sewed. After we sewed and stuffed our puppets, Mrs. Hans took them to a lady to have faces painted on professionally. I still have my "Witchy-Poo." Unfortunately, we were never able to go beyond finishing the marionettes to perform a play, as we all moved to seventh grade and to a different teacher before the puppets were ready. The project got too big and time ran out, but it was fun to do and we learned a lot while doing it.

Our teachers David Merkel taught band, Miss Flynn taught choir, Mr. Vaughn taught English, and Mr. Riley taught algebra. These teachers were right up there as "favorites" too. They were "saints" in my book. Mrs. Olds and Mr. Riley will never be forgotten. Thank you!

I was an A-, B+ student, but I never could figure out how an A or B or C could be a number. Mr. Riley was giving tests on the last day of school. He gave us six tests, and I was the only one left taking the sixth test. Everyone else had turned in their papers and left. I was still there trying to pass, when I heard Mr. Riley speak up. "Janice, come up to my desk. You have done everything I've asked. You were here every day, have taken all the tests, and you still do not get algebra. For your effort and for not giving up, I am giving you a C+. Thanks again, Mr. Riley!

When I was in the twelfth grade, the school offered advanced sewing. I asked if I could get into the class.

The teacher asked why I had not been in her other three. I said that my other classes would not let me, and that I was a "pinch and dump cook. "I had already made aprons on Mom's sewing machine, but I needed to learn to make button holes, how to adjust patterns, match plaids, etc. I tried to convince her that I needed more advanced stuff.

"Okay," she said. "You can come to class tomorrow. I am running a test the first day. If you pass the test you can stay."

So, I went. The next day, the teacher gave us material and told us to make a skirt. I want a waistband, a hem, and a button hole sewed by hand. Long story short, I passed with a B+ and I had never been in her class before.

CHAPTER 16: BOB

I first met my friend, Bob Emerick, at class in eighth grade. We were friends until the tenth grade. We started to date off and on, finally went steady, which led to engagement and marriage in 1958. Bob was a big part of my last school years. His family had a farm, but his father was very sick. Bob had to do the farm work, go to school and do school work as well. We dated once a week and rarely talked on the phone. It was too hard to talk on the phone system we had. Bob had come from a one-room school, named Spencer School on Barlow Road South of M-72. He felt lost when he came to our school. The school was huge to him.

Dating was hard because he lived 34 miles, one-way, from me. Then, after picking me up, we would drive 25 miles to Oscoda or Tawas or eleven miles to Hale, after which, Bob would still need to drive home. There wasn't much to do in Hale after the movie, so we usually went to Tawas or watched our wonderful rolling-up-and-down black-and-white television.

We were also part of both school plays. Bob was the leading man in both, I did box office one year, and was a prompter for the other. I helped with a lot of things that I was asked to do. I would not take a better part in the play because I got stage-fright so badly. Not any more though! Thank heavens, because the stage fright was awful. I would know something well but couldn't say anything because all I could see were eyes watching me.

Once when I was sixteen, Bob came over to visit. Consumers Power pulled the water way down to repair the front of the dam, which lowered the water so much we had mud plains in many places. All the logs and stumps held sinkers and artificial bait, hooks, swivels, and leaders. We were like pirates that day. We came home with a pail full of treasures. We even found a logger's lunch unopened. They used to carry canned fish for a quick safe lunch. This one was sardines, a flat can that could be opened by turn a key to peal a small strip of the can back and around the key.

We looked at the can and thought maybe he fell in and lost his life there. It didn't seem right for us to take it. We looked at each other and put it back where we found it, still unopened.

We were near the area called Blue Rock by the loggers. That rock was always causing trouble for them, so they painted it blue. It was too big to move. Consumer's Power was going to build another dam in the area because this was a real fast part of the River. It was between Five Channels and Loud dams. As it turned out, the two dams did the job and another did not need to be built.

It was my cookie recipe that made my boyfriend interested in me. He knew a cook when he saw one and I was it. One morning, I decided to bake a large batch of cookies. These were called date-nut cookies. The recipe used dates, walnuts, and brown sugar. In the afternoon, I was getting the cookies ready to bake, and Dad was getting ready for work on the 4:00 shift. He looked at what I was doing and asked what I was baking. I told him I was making date and nut cookies. He simply said, "See you tomorrow."

Later, Bob came over and we watched movies on T.V. The reception was good that night and there was a good line up to watch. He did not have a T.V. at home yet. While watching T.V., we ate a dish of cookies. When the dish was empty, I filled it up again. Bob said he really loved them and ate these up as well. At the time, he could really eat. Soon the second plateful was gone. I asked if he could eat more. Bob simply replied, "Boy, those are really good!" I went for the last plateful, and he polished those off, too. He left for home with a very full stomach that night. Bob later said it was a long way home that night because shortly he felt very tired. He had hauled hay all day, which was hard. To date me, he had to drive 35 miles through the woods one way, then he be up to milk cows at 5:30 a.m.

"Where in the world did you hide the cookies?" Dad asked me the next morning. "I looked all over the kitchen and could not find them."

I admitted that Bob had eaten them all.

"What!" Dad said, "Don't they feed him at home." Bob and I have often laughed about that night over the years. I have always said my cookies caught a wonderful man for me.

Oscoda area schools had a lot of money from Government grants for children in their school district from Consumer's Power, the Wurtsmith Air Base, from personal property taxes and taxes. The school system supported many classes that other C-level schools could not. We had a concert band, marching band, choir, boys' and girls' basketball, football, drama, boxing, debate, FFA, and trips.

In the seventh grade, I went with the other seventh graders to Tiger Stadium to watch a baseball game. We were sitting behind home plate and saw everything up close. It had a fence over the area so no balls came into our area. We had sold fudge made at home and other candies to earn some of the money. We worked hard at this for many weeks. I'm sure that we had help getting 65 children down to the game. We went by school bus.

In the eleventh grade, we had to find our own way to Bay City to see a Shakespeare play. Bob and I went to see that one together for a date. Everything went ok. The play had some real costumes that came from community area groups. Another car load of girls went as well. It made Shakespeare come alive for me and I started to understand it more. The play was Midsummer Night's Dream.

When the play ended, we walked out to a blizzard. It was a terrible drive home. Bob and I thought about staying a motel overnight, but it would have meant two rooms to rent since we were not married. Oh boy, people would have loved to spread that story around school! The girls in the other car did just that and shared the room together.

Bob and I trucked home and came up M-65 to Loud Dam Road and kept going, sometimes through snow drifts. When we finally got to our house, I made Bob call home and tell his parents he was spending the night with us. He was to milk the cows in the morning. I got him all set in our spare room, and in the morning, I told Mom that Bob had slept in our spare room. She was glad he had. There sure were a lot of questions from the other six girls when we went back to school.

Our senior class worked from eleventh to twelfth grade so that all of us could go on a class trip. The trip started out on a bus from school in Oscoda, very early Sunday morning. We went to church in Detroit, some place where a Methodist and a Catholic church were across the street from each other, before boarding the boat. Everyone had to be a Methodist or a Catholic that day. The teachers had us line up according to our preference and went to church coming back the same way. From here, we went to the area where the S. S. American was waiting for our group. There were other classes there from other schools. We were headed for Mackinac Island and on to Chicago.

Bob and I had fun, or at least I did traveling along and eating aboard the ship. We played games and they had prizes. Bob was ready to get off in three hours. Once he walked all over the boat that was it for him. The boys were in one area and the girls in another, but Bob and I would meet for lunch and supper. We had a half day on Mackinaw Island and then we were back on the boat for Chicago.

We stayed in one of the top hotels in Chicago and went to the Museum of Science and Industry. It was so big that we were running to see as much as we could. We skipped some areas so we could spend more time at the next thing to see. Bob and I went to the Empire Room for supper. We were two very green teenagers. A man was at the door who said "Hi," and we walked in and sat down. Now, we had three people by us. That seemed unusual but we still hadn't caught on. The first man had been the doorman, whom we should have tipped for finding us a table. A second man brought water, and the third one had the menus. I took a menu and looked at the prices. This was 1956, and there wasn't anything we could afford to eat. I quietly said to Bob, "We can't afford to eat here!" I stood up, looked at the three men, and said, "I think we made a mistake coming in here. We are on a class trip and cannot afford this." Then, I headed for the door. At the door I turned and said, "I'm sorry." We left feeling dumb, but it was an experience.

CHAPTER 17: PEGGY THE DOG

One year, my Aunt Kay came up with a tiny toy terrier puppy. I had always wanted a dog. I was in school so much the puppy turned into family dog. She loved us all. She was black and white with two brown spots over her eyes. We called her "Peggy." Peggy was a nice dog until Mom blew up the canner on the stove. Never put apples with the skins on in a pressure cooker. In this case, Mom had done all the checks, but there happened to be a skin across the vent. So when Mom removed the lid, "Boom!" The cooker exploded upward and sideways because of the pressure. Unfortunately, Peggy's bed was right by the stove, and she got piping hot applesauce on her tail, her back, and in her bed with her. She ended up with more spots, sores and scabs that healed slowly, as did Mom in the areas where she got applesauce on her. Thankfully, both recovered well and Peggy lived for a long time, even after Bob and I got married. She was pretty old when Mom and Dad had to put her down.

GOING AWAY BUT COMING BACK

About a week after graduation, I started looking for a job in Oscoda, Tawas and Tawas City. I was ready to move on, but I soon found out that there weren't any jobs available. I wanted to work close to home. Being with Bob every weekend would have been nice. I was still young, too, and many places said that I would need to be at least 17. I stayed home during the summer, waiting until fall months when I was turning 17 to go to Saginaw. I more or less skipped Kindergarten because of nursery school. I was sent for social interaction with others. I had learned my ABCs in nursery school.

Bob would drive over once a week from his home on Clemens Road to date me. Sometimes he had to call to tell me they were putting up hay or combining wheat or oats and couldn't come. So, sometimes it was two or three weeks before we met up again.

That fall, I finally got a job, actually two jobs on the same day, the day before I turned 17. I had made about three trips to Saginaw to see about jobs before, but they turned me down. Soon, two places hired me on the same day. The first job was at the loading dock in Saginaw and

I cannot remember the name of the dock. I was happy that I had my job. Before Mom and I left town, we checked one more time at Michigan Bell, and they hired me, too. I knew I would be warm in the winter and cool in the summer at Bell, so that's the one I went with. Mom drove me back to the loading dock to tell the man who hired me that I had found another job and wouldn't be working there. He blew his stack. He swore at me and used a lot of nasty words. I spoke up, said I was sorry that it hadn't worked out, thanked him for his trouble, and walked out. He was still yelling. I was very happy to see what my almost boss was really like, as he showed me his true colors for handling people.

Off to Saginaw I went to work for Michigan Bell. As I had no car, I made a date with the greyhound bus to take me to Saginaw on Sunday's and home on Friday's after work. The first time I went up those Greyhound steps to work in Saginaw, I was scared. I was leaving Mom, Dad, Bob, and the AuSable River for the city! City life was strange to me. I was always looking around and checking to see if I was in safe territory. I wondered if I could make it there. I told myself, you must, because I knew what I wanted.

Bob and I had to work a while to save money for our marriage. We had an unused hired-hand house next to Bob's family home. His folks had rented it to a little old lady for a small fee because they no longer hired men to work the farm. She didn't have money for a larger place so she lived in that house until the spring of 1958. Bob and I waited for the house to become available. I rented a room at the YMCA and worked in Saginaw from fall of 1956 to May 1958. I found out that cities can be lonely places, too.

My last trip home on the Greyhound was the happiest ride of all. I was going home to fresh air and the loving environment I had grown up with. I had never found that peace and comfort in the city. In fact, living in the city was not the adventure I thought it would be. I was going home to marry Bob. I was starting on another new life, marriage and farming. Bob and I were married, June 7, 1958.

CHAPTER 18: ENDINGS

Today, our old dam-site house looks defeated and lonely. Many of the trees have been cut down. The house looks hunched-down somehow. It's now painted grey. How depressing is that? My heart was broken when I saw the house like that. Consumer's Power, now known as Consumer's Energy, always maintained those homes, doing repairs, upgrading the phones, and re-painting inside and out. They hired different contractors to do the work.

When I was around 12, Mom and Dad bought 10 acres near Hale on M-65. They wanted to build their retirement home there. Later, they sold the ten acres when they moved to Mikado, Michigan. The land near M-65, was all wooded and they had brushed-out the center for the house. They worked at it a lot, and I spent a few days on it, too.

After Dad began thinking about retirement, Mom and Dad moved to Glennie to take a caretaking job. Mom got a job there, too. They saved their money, as Dad still drove to Loud Dam each day to work his shift from Glennie. It was about six years after they moved to

Glennie that Dad had his first heart attack. He was getting ready for work when it came on. Mom called his supervisor at Five Channels Dam and told him that she was taking Dad to the hospital in Tawas. Dad had another heart attack in the hospital. After Dad had his heart attacks, he retired from the Dams. Six years later, they moved from Glennie to Mikado, so they would be closer to Bob and me. This was the first home that they had ever owned. They had rented the Consumers Power house, and the house in Flint. They owned the little house but it was like a cabin and not a home.

Consumer's Power never forgot the dedication these men had working at the dams on those schedules. All the men had issues with their health because of working swing shifts for years. Mom and I were surprised at Dad's funeral. Consumer's Power sent a man up to present Mom with a Bible in a wooden box. This was very much a surprise because by then Dad had been retired for a long time. This just shows how much that company thought of their men. This is being written years later, I want to say thank you, again, to Consumers Power.

EPILOGUE
SPIRIT OF THE AUSABLE

The Native American Indian saw the AuSable and thought the River was a spiritual place. It is for me, too. Whenever I cross over the River bridges today in a car or when I stand on her banks beside her ever-flowing waters, I feel a renewing healing through her waters. It's a spiritual experience that I can only try to tell you about.

She is a river of life, peace, and home right down to my soul. She's larger and stronger than any of us. She was put here by God shaping the land for man's use. We need to treat her with respect, keep trash out of her, and remember that whatever we take in, we must take out. We need to keep her waters pure for future generations to enjoy.

The AuSable River

AFTERWARD

This book was fun to write. It has been fun to remember my carefree youth growing up. I thought everyone was growing up in the same environment as I was until I spoke to a historian from Oscoda. I found out that life on the AuSable River Dams was a lot different than what most experienced and that no one had written about it. Through this book, I have tried to take readers back into my world in the 1940s and 50s. I always wanted to write my insights about that life. As I wrote, I realized how much that life revolved around the men and their shift work. It was a hard life for the men, too, shifting from working one week on days, one week on afternoons, and one on midnights, followed by one week off. The men did this month after month. The changing sleep-wake pattern soon took its toll on them all, and on family life in general. Would I ever want to live that way again? No! It would be too hard, but I still love car rides these days!

I never dreamed I would every write a book. I thought about this for a long time. I did it because of the way life is going. I wanted to create a life history of what it was like to live in a company house with a father as a hydro-operator. Those dam houses are private now and the dams are automated, so this life is gone forever.

The people from our class of 1956 seem to be closer to each other than those from other years. We were more like brothers and sisters, and we all seem to enjoy getting together for class reunions when we can. We started having them every five years after graduation. Then we moved to getting together once a year, usually in July. In 2017, there were only a few of us left so we simply went out to dinner. I like attending our class reunions. They are a real joy. It is great to see classmates again, and catch up on their life. I have wondered why our class has such a close relationship. Was it the hard times after the Depression and the war? Was it the fear of polio, with the death of Carol Robinson in the fifth grade and Shirley Brown contracting polio in the seventh that made us feel close? The reunions bring us all back to the way life was growing up.

The following information is from the Forest Service brochure about Lumberman's Monument (Page 9).

An incident in a lumber camp years ago gave R.G. Schreck of East Tawas, former supervisor of the Huron National Forest, the idea of creating a monument suitable, lasting tribute to perpetuate the memory of Michigan lumbermen. He assumed the initiative and got things started. For several years, Mr. Schreck worked on getting support from well-to-do lumberjacks to bring his idea to life. Finally, on May 29, 1929, he was able to gather together a group of men who represented the principal lumbering families of Michigan at the Holland Hotel in East Tawas. Each of them was interested in the plan and, before the day was over, unanimously accepted the proposed location of the monument. Collections started coming in at once. By March 1930, $44,000 had been collected from lumbermen throughout Michigan.

There were various ideas for the type of monument to be erected, including one for a tower of bells. Finally, the decision was to have three bronze figures, nine feet tall: one a sawyer with an ax and saw; a river driver with a peavey; and a timber cruiser with a compass. Robert

Aitkins of New York City was picked to make the monument. His contract was for $50,000, and his second model of the figures was accepted. Mr. Aitkins drew on photos of a person standing on the exact site chosen for the monument.

The spot picked was owned by Consumer's Power and the US Government. To get the deed for the property, Consumer's had to quit-claim the property to the Government. But the Government could not accept it as a sale that way. Both entities had to convey the land to the Northeastern Michigan Development Bureau, with the understanding that when Consumer's Power could release the land from a trust deed, or trust mortgage, the land would be conveyed to the United States. The Monument was landscaped by the Civilian Conservation Corp (CCC). The words "Aitkin Fecit" that appear on the Monument mean, literally, "Aitkin made it." *Fecit* comes from the Latin verb meaning "to do" or "to make." The completed Monument was dedicated on July 16, 1932.

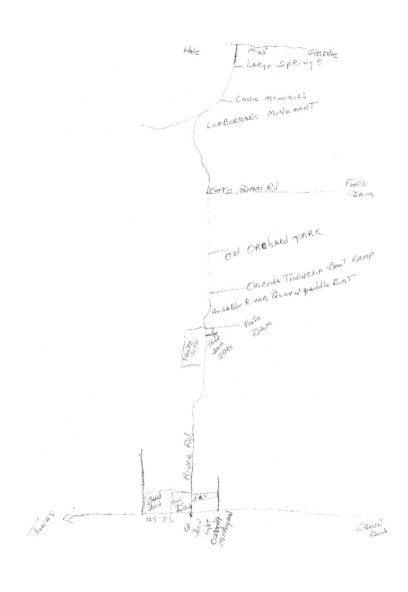

ACKNOWLEDGEMENTS AND THANK YOU

This book is for the teachers and the classmates of 1956, as they were all my brothers and sisters helping me learn in the long days and nights away from home, thank you also to Mom and Dad.

Thanks, too, to my husband, Robert Emerick, who helped me a lot, to my three daughters who supported and encouraged me: Katherine Thompson who helped to edit my book, Anita Mardney who edited and published my book for me, and Susan Maturen who wrote the poem called "The River" many years before this book. Thanks to my two Sons-in Law, Randy Thompson and Mike Maturen, who do so much for both Bob and I. Thanks to my seven grandchildren: Michael and Laura Thompson, Jessica and Jeremy Hood, Joshua and Brooke Maturen, Jeremy and Errin Maturen, Rebekah Maturen, Madison and London Mardney. Thanks to my great grandchildren Aiden Thompson, Matthew and Tyler Cutting and brother Conner Hood, Emma Maturen, Wyatt Maturen, Charlotte Grace Desotell.

Thanks to the Alcona author's group for their direction and encouragement. I learned a lot with them. When I first went to the group, I wasn't sure that I could write a book. Along the way, perhaps on the sixth re-write I was still waffling about writing it. It was a hard job getting all of this information out of my brain and to put to paper. Now, here I am at the end and right or wrong we are going to publish.

Thanks to Mary Ann Crawford the teacher of our writers' group, who edited my first draft and made it read like a book, suggested I include maps and gave many ideas to me.

Thanks, as well, to the Hydro Reporter for the help and information when I asked for it. I used to read the magazine when waiting for Dad to finish his shift at the Dam through the years. I asked if I could get a copy of what they wrote about the dams and what was happening with them. Because I was a Dam kid, they said yes!

Researched from:

Alcona County Herald

Alcona County Review

Materials given to me by Val Fredrickson

Consumers Energy's material about Loud Dam in the "Hydro Reporter"

U.S. Forest Services' Brochure on Lumberman's Monument

Donna Janice and Robert (Bob) Emerick
A friendship, love, and match made in heaven!

ABOUT THE AUTHOR

Donna Janice Emerick was born in 1938 in Flint, Michigan. When she was 3-1/2 years old, her parents, Donald and Helen Weinberg, moved to the AuSable River to live in a Consumers Power Company House at Loud Dam. She grew up in the north woods, the only girl of her age in her area. She had no brothers or sisters. She married her high school sweetheart, Robert L. Emerick, two years after graduation in 1956. At this time, they took over the the Emerick family farm. They watched their farm become a Michigan Centennial Farm in 1984. They have been married over 61 years and raised three wonderful daughters, Kathy, Anita, and Susan.

She has thought about writing the book of her life on the River for many years and now it happened!

Made in the USA
Middletown, DE
28 February 2020